to Mar

Awesome Footsteps

—Psalm 37:23

A Missionary's Memoirs

The True Tales Trilogy

Part III

By Michael J. Hawron

Pleasure to meet you!

— Mike Hawron
9/29/18
Decatur, TX

Awesome Footsteps

© 2018 by Michael J. Hawron.

All Biblical references are from the King James Version.

This is a work of creative nonfiction. The stories told in this book are true and portrayed to the best of the author's memory. Some details may not be exactly factual: some events are compressed; some characters are composite; the recollection of exact wording of conversations and minor details is not always possible. Some names and identifying details have been changed to protect the privacy of individuals.

Foreword

To the avowed atheists among us, I will honestly suggest that this book is probably not really for you. There may be too many references to a Supreme Creator, spiritual values and answered prayers for your comfort zone. Since my basic premise is unacceptable to your worldview, you will dismiss me as merely another "religious moron," even though I have a measured IQ of 162, attended MIT and have a Master of Science degree in Higher Education.

To the agnostics among you, I heartily say: "Welcome!" I believe this book will give you much interesting food for thought, as you make up your own mind as to what is or isn't true in the universe.

To those of you who have deeply-held personal beliefs and convictions, this book should serve to reinforce, affirm and encourage you in your faith. As in my two previous books, all of the stories told herein are true, even those which have no clear earthly explanation. People of faith—all faiths— these days are all too regularly subjected to ridicule, abuse, discrimination, litigation and finally persecution for their "crime" of failing to worship at the twin altars of moral relativism and secular cynicism.

While the modern non-spiritual individual finds the truth in Hans Christian Andersen's tale, *The Emperor's New Clothes,* to be self-evident, the same individual fails to see the folly in today's pervasive judgement-by-collective-narcissism.

When I speak of "belief," I refer to personally held convictions of universal spiritual truths and principles. I am not referring to handed-down traditions that have been accepted and mindlessly aped without proper reflection. Herein is the vital difference between the individual who truly is thoughtfully spiritual, as compared to one who is dogmatically or blindly religious. I salute the former, and encourage the latter to reconsider their ways.

Michael J. Hawron

Autumn 2017

Dedication

The first book in this series, *Entertaining Detours*, was mainly about **my** various humorous mishaps and adventures while traversing the globe in earlier days.

The second volume, *The Little Town with the Big Heart*, was mostly about **others**: the wonderful, good people—past and present—of New Boston, in East Texas.

This concluding volume of my **True Tales Trilogy** celebrates the **unseen personage** who has made all these events possible, "for in him we live, and move, and have our being."—Acts 17:28.

As such, there was a ghost writer of sorts for this new book—*the* **author** *and finisher of our faith*—Hebrews 12:2.

Pastors and Sunday school teachers may find some of the dozens of short stories contained herein to be helpful, vivid illustrations of the lessons they are trying to impart.

Table of Contents

The steps of a good man are ordered by the Lord:
and he delighteth in his way.

—Psalm 37:23

1.

*For I know the thoughts that I think
toward you, saith the Lord, thoughts of
peace, and not of evil, to give you an
expected end.*

—*Jeremiah 29:11*

I had a very peaceful dream. Then I awoke to a cool, crisp, sunny autumn day in Cambridge, Massachusetts. There were two remarkable features about this situation. One was the vivid content of the dream, which I will reveal in a moment. The second, and more significant feature, was that the dream was very pleasant. I was usually plagued with nightmares and could not remember the last time I had experienced a nice dream, probably not since I was a young child. Now I was a freshman at MIT, a little country kid in the big city for the very first time.

As a child, I had been raised Catholic by my very devout mother, going to Mass or Novena several times each week. Religion was mysterious, yet familiar and comfortable. When we attended the midweek Mass in the quaint stone chapel of the Franciscan monks just off Washington Avenue, where the new I-90 was just emerging, I felt I was in my safe space. I was wholehearted in my religious pursuit, and followed along with my Missal in Latin, eventually memorizing every word of the liturgy.

I discovered that there were special prayers of indulgence written down for the penitent, which offered hundreds, if not thousands, of years' grace off one's future time in purgatory if said during a moment of pure grace—such as right after communion on a First Saturday, before casting a lustful glance at the pretty girl in the next pew. It seemed like free shopping to me, so I racked up as many years as I could. One could not have too many, it would appear, since this waiting period in the afterlife was deemed limitless. I had hundreds of thousands of years stashed away long before my first acne spots appeared.

Fast forward and now as a young man, I was about to go through the painful metamorphosis from religious to spiritual. At liberal, science-based MIT, I faced new headwinds of challenges to my belief system. "*Why* do you go to Mass?" challenged Ed, my roommate—a professing atheist—during one of our frequent intellectual debates. It would not be sophisticated enough for me to reply "Because my parents always went," or "Because the Church teaches that you will go to Hell if you don't."

Deep down I knew that I needed a solid answer that stemmed from personal conviction, not from mindless tradition. Complicating matters, I had what those espousing the Transformative Theory of adult learning call a "disorienting dilemma." That would be when a strongly held aspect of one's beliefs or value system was suddenly turned on its head, no longer incontrovertible. Where I grew up, in North Greenbush, there was little controversial or upsetting. To demonstrate, I could remember the big scandal that arose when an *Italian* family built a nice new house and moved into our neighborhood, across the street from my Uncle Frank's place. I didn't see the crime in associating with such people, so I went and introduced myself, welcoming them to our quiet little street. I was glad I did, as their daughter was quite cute.

At MIT, I suddenly found myself living amongst folks I had only *read* about in books before—blacks and Pakistanis, Russians and Chinese, seemingly-manly women and—apparently—gay priests. One evening after a heated discussion with my roommate Ed, the last straw fell. The faculty sponsor for our dorm floor knocked on my door one Saturday night when most of my other fellow students were out elsewhere partying. The Dutch priest, who said Mass at the little campus chapel I attended faithfully each Sunday, was there in my doorway, smiling and ready for an evening of romance, it seemed.

A wide array of emotions hit me simultaneously: shock, embarrassment, fear, betrayal, confusion, anger and a deep sense of loss. My frame of reference had been shattered. The structure I had embraced for protection was instead now threatening me and my belief system. I cannot remember what I said, if anything, in response to the priest's overture. I remember closing the door as quickly and firmly as my trembling hands allowed. One thing was certain, however: I could not attend Mass the next morning and be face-to-face with this same person. This meant that for the first time in my life, I willingly chose not to attend Sunday services. I had been taught *that* act of defiance was a mortal (unforgiveable) sin.

Conflicted, I lay on my bed for hours, unable to find release in the drug of sleep. The Church had taught that we mere mortals were not eloquent enough in our own right to approach the Throne of Grace with our own words, so many written prayers were helpfully supplied that covered a whole range of events and situations. For years I had secretly rebelled against this pronouncement and tried mixing a few words of my own amongst the memorized prayers I recited. Now this rebellion would prove useful to my peace of mind.

My handmade prayer went something like this: *Dear Lord, I know that not going to Mass might condemn me to Hell. But I cannot attend Mass tomorrow and face that priest! I just need some time to sort things out. I realize I'm leaving myself open to being struck dead tonight for my willfulness. But if you could cut me some slack, I would really appreciate it. You know that I do love You, and Your Church.*

With those words I drifted off to sleep, not knowing if I had taken my last breath on earth. At the very least, I was fairly certain I was in for a nasty nightmare. To my surprise, I awoke after a very beautiful dream which left me with a warm, peaceful and welcoming feeling.

In my dream it was late afternoon on a glorious spring day as the sun, low on the horizon, cast surrealistically long shadows down the hillside of a big city park. I was strolling with some people I did not recognize, yet there seemed to be some strong bond of camaraderie. I was at peace, and I felt loved. Somehow I knew this dream was an answer to my prayer the previous night.

Soon I forgot the dream as I got busy with studies and all the stuff young men do while away from home at college. While I had fun, and was successful in my classes, there pervaded an empty sensation, and lack of clear vision for my future. A year and a half later, I was a sophomore and still struggling to finalize my choice of degree major. I was interested in many things, but felt frightened to commit to something I wasn't sure that I wanted to do for the rest of my life.

College life in the Boston area in the early '70s was a kaleidoscope of radical causes, rock music, anti-war protests, mindless capers and myriad forms of proselytizing. All actions have their own natural consequences. One night I was beginning to feel the unbearable weight of the consequence of my own actions on my young adult shoulders. I found myself desperately praying wholeheartedly—something I had not done before. I put forth a great deal of effort, asking something to this effect: *God, if you can help me with all these problems, and show me a better way to live my life, I will follow.*

The next day, not thinking much about my prayer, I went about my day of classes, working at my part-time job, listening to my music, and so on. Around noon, I bumped into a couple of hippies on campus. There was always a flow of free spirits along the Charles River basin which Harvard and MIT share. Sometimes those free spirits had brownies or cookies to offer which were extra tasty. I did not know what these two strangers wanted, but they seemed friendly enough. They invited me to see a movie they were showing that evening across campus.

When it grew dark enough so the lights from the Boston skyscrapers reflected off the mirror-still surface of the Charles River, I headed down the three flights of stairs from my corner room at the dorm. I painfully hobbled across campus, leaning clumsily on the crutches I had never quite mastered as I slowly covered the half-mile walk.

I had been using crutches since Christmas, as I had damaged my knee tobogganing with old high school friends during the winter break. The rest of my body had twisted around 180 degrees while my left foot had remained stuck in place in the deep snow. Now I could not properly bend my leg and I was quite frustrated and depressed by my first-ever experience of limitations on my movements. I had just learned that the painful x-ray process where a large amount of dye had been injected into my knee to expand the parts for better definition had to be repeated. The equipment wasn't set correctly and the results were out of focus. Salt in the wound, as it were.

Exhausted from my efforts, and chilled by the cold night air, I collapsed into the first available seat at the back of the room. Some folks came by to say hello and then the room darkened and the movie reel began spinning. I was expecting to see some sort of counter-culture movie. Instead I was confronted with a documentary where a succession of individuals described their faith in God. I was furious! I felt I had been tricked. I was already jaded by the seemingly endless parade of Hare Krishna and Campus Crusade and Students for a Democratic Society (SDS) on campus, all self-righteously pitching their own special solutions to the world's problem.

Much as I wanted to, I could not just get up and leave. It would take me some time to gather enough strength for the journey back to my dorm room. So I sat there, trapped, fuming and ready to argue at the first opportunity. Instead, an hour later, I found myself praying after someone had explained the plan of salvation to me. My mind was so reeling from this sudden sequence of events that I was halfway home before I realized I was walking normally and had left my crutches back at the meeting room. I no longer needed them! The pain in my knee was gone.

A few weeks later, late afternoon on a glorious spring day, the sun, low on the horizon, cast outlandishly long shadows down the hillside of the Boston Common. I was strolling with some new friends—fellow believers in the Christian faith—when suddenly I froze in my steps and exclaimed ecstatically. The beauty of the scene; the warm camaraderie of my friends; the exact details of each tree, squirrel and park-goer all conspired perfectly to propel me into a déjà-vu shock: I had dreamt this exact scenario eighteen months prior!

Thus began my life of faith, something I had not planned and had never anticipated. All of the stories in this book are true. They are not intended to draw attention to any specialness on my part. My intention is to demonstrate the faithfulness of our Creator, and the effective power of belief.

2.

Unto me every knee shall bow

—Isaiah 45:23

*O*ut of the mouths of babes and sucklings hast
thou ordained strength, declared the psalmist
David. He should know, having himself once
impertinently slain a giant when he was just a young
lad. Brand-new to the faith, I had just attended a
class about the early Christians in the Book of Acts
of the Bible. There it was explained to me that circa
30 A.D., some ordinary men and women did
extraordinary deeds solely on the authority and
strength of the name of their recently martyred
Savior, Jesus Christ.

There was about to be an exam covering this
material but no paper or pencils were provided. For
no logical explanation, I found myself in a very poor
and dangerous part of Boston, on Symphony Road.
Walking along the narrow, gray sidewalk, I had to
step around the body of a recently departed resident
of the neighborhood which blocked my progress.
The murder weapon (a knife) was still implanted
firmly into the victim's back. One did not stop to ask
questions in such locations. To escape that view, I
cut through the Symphony Road Community Garden,

a green patch of relief amidst the aging brick tenement buildings, heading south to Public Alley 810.

Thinking I'd escaped the fire, I found myself in the frying pan instead. As my friend and I walked along the park's narrow pathway, we were suddenly confronted by this great, huge gorilla of a man who exploded out of the tall bushes, towering over us. He spoke loudly, slurring his words, high on something. "Give me yer money!" he demanded.

We had walked right into a trap. Our forward progress was blocked. My legs had turned to Jell-O and were of no use to me in an escape bid. I would have gladly handed over my money, but for the fact that I did not have a dime on me at the time. "We don't have any money!" I pleaded. That response provoked an angry roar. "What do you *mean*, 'you don't have *any* money'?" Out came a scary knife. "I *cut* people for *less* than that!" he boasted malevolently. I believed him.

"*What* kind of people *are* you anyways—you don't have *any* money!? What do you *do*, without money?" he questioned, at the same time both curious and frustrated. *Scared-to-death-kind-of-people, that's who we are,* I thought to myself. I knew I couldn't fight this mugger and I seemed to be too petrified to run or to scream. (Screaming seemed like a bad idea anyways.) The only thing that came to mind was that Acts of the Apostles class I had just had.

Summoning up whatever remaining strength and resolve I still possessed, I yelled as loudly and as boldly as I could, "We just tell folks about **Jesus**! That's all!" At that point I imagined my life was pretty much over, about to be sliced in two by that large knife buried in the filthy paw of this menacing monster. *I'll go to Heaven*, I thought somewhat comfortingly.

When the knife did not strike and the roaring had suddenly stopped, I dared to open my eyes. Our attacker had his two hands around his *own* thick throat, as if *he* were being chocked by a pair of unseen hands. He was sputtering and gurgling something fierce, wildly staggering towards us. Then he fell over into the bushes, landing prone and gasping for breath.

Suddenly my legs began working again and we ran for all that we were worth, never once looking back. That evening at our Bible study group, we had a really big story to tell. "This 'name of Jesus' stuff really works!"

3.

*In a dream, in a vision of the night,
when deep sleep falleth upon men, in
slumberings upon the bed; Then He
openeth the ears of men, and sealeth
their instruction.*

—Job 33:15-16

The following happened to me early on in my walk of faith. Nothing quite like this has ever happened since then. I feel the experience was meant as an encouraging sign from a benevolent parent above for a well-meaning child who then was struggling to find his way. The child, once grown, is then expected to carry on without such overt support.

I first landed as a brand-new missionary in New Zealand just prior to my 21st birthday, leaving Upstate New York mid-July for the 27-hour flight (before the days of 747s) and traveling to what I considered to be a "south sea island."

I packed mainly light clothing, and threw in a thin green windbreaker for good measure. I obviously had not paid sufficient attention in world geography class, as July in Auckland is the dead of winter in the Southern Hemisphere and it was very chilly, with evening temperatures hovering just above freezing.

We had a Christian coffee shop of sorts with a wood fire going in the meeting room fireplace, and that was the only source of heat in the entire building. For the next couple months, I usually never strayed far from that hearth, and I happily volunteered to secure all the necessary firewood. This arrangement led to a rather interesting experience that I will leave to the metaphysicists to explain.

Three months prior, I had been in Boston, Massachusetts, where one of those overly spiritual type folks challenged me to try an exercise: I was supposed to be seriously curious as to what would happen 90 days hence and to pray for some dream as a sign.

That night I did, in fact, have a vivid vision in my sleep wherein I seemed to be picking through the aftermath of a large destructive fire. There were burnt or charred timbers everywhere I looked. I could not accurately gauge distances in the dream, of course, so I dramatically concluded the holocaust's reach must have been global, or at least nationwide, in its scope. Within a few days, life uneventfully proceeded as normal and I forgot all about that strange, unsettling dream.

Now let's fast forward to a cold morning in the Auckland inner city suburb of Ponsonby where I was out gathering some wood scraps to feed my precious comfort-sustaining fire. There had been a fire at an old, wooden schoolhouse nearby where I found some wood that had survived that fire, ready to be gathered up for today's new fire in our little fireplace.

As I surveyed the scene looking for more available fuel, I was suddenly déjà vu-ed into the remarkably identical scenario of my dream from three months prior. I asked Simon, the Kiwi chap who was with me, what the date was and sure enough, it was exactly three months to the day since that weird dream I had had in Boston, some 8,000 miles away.

4.

*But my God shall supply all your need
according to his riches in glory by
Christ Jesus.*

—Philippians 4:19

The life of faith as missionaries often came down to a matter of dollars and cents. We preached the Gospel full time, and often overtime, but there was never a steady paycheck each week. Paying bills each month was a regular challenge, and rigorous budgeting was essential.

Sometimes, out of the blue, a letter would arrive unexpectedly from a church congregation, friend, or relative with a donation enclosed. More than once, it was the exact amount needed to complete some payment. Some donations were more unusual . . .

Later, when living in Queensland, Australia, shortly after the birth of Suzy, my first daughter, our mission home was in a bind, of sorts. We decided to take action to rise above the hand-to-mouth practice of buying food items the day we needed them, in whatever quantity we could afford. Small quantities were always more expensive. If we could budget and buy a month's supply of staples ahead of time, in bulk, we could stretch our valuable dollars much further. We calculated that we needed $100 in order to purchase a month's worth of dry goods.

We set the target date for one fortnight later, and proceeded with various fundraising efforts. We prayed specifically that we would have $100 by the time we went shopping. One of our team arranged to borrow a relative's van for that day. After those fourteen days, however, we had raised just enough money for the gas. There was of course, a strong sense of disappointment. While unspoken, there was also a very palpable sentiment of confused disbelief. *How could this be? We prayed in faith and acted on our prayers.*

Before really thinking the matter through, I blurted out, "Let's go anyways! We have the van, let's just see what happens!" Off we headed to the bulk food store without any money . . .

Along the drive, I thought I'd spotted a $20 bill by the side of the road. The Australian $20 bill is bright orange, and I was certain I had spotted something that size, shape and color. We pulled to the curb, and everyone jumped out to search. It turned out to be only a discarded candy wrapper.

At this point I was feeling doubly stupid—first for suggesting we go shopping without any money, and now this latest feat, of claiming to find money that did not exist. Often in the faith life, moments of hopelessness or embarrassment strike just before a prayer is answered.

This was certainly one of those moments. Now, at the risk of appearing totally nonsensical, I stated that since we already had the car stopped, I would look around some more. Soon I spotted a *real* $20 bill! Someone else found another. I found a third. A fourth orange $20 bill was found. Then, under a parked car, I spotted a fifth. It was suggested we keep searching, but in my heart I had the quiet assurance that there were no more to be found. Others kept searching, but found nothing. We needed $100, and that was exactly how much we found.

Next, I proceeded to pour water on the sacrifice. (See 1st Kings, Chapter 18.) Right near where we were parked was a police station. I walked in, clutching the $100 that had just been found, and declared, "We just found $100 out on the street. Has anyone reported any money missing?"

"No mate! It's yours! Go on your way!" was the officer's reply.

To me, these were the second and third miracles of that moment: that I would walk into the police station, willing to surrender the money that we had just found; and that the police would quickly and firmly advise that we should keep it! We happily complied.

And in that inglorious and circuitous manner, our grand scheme to raise $100 to buy a month's supply of dry goods was fulfilled. I have shopped for food thousands of times since then, but never have I felt such a divine connection between my shopping list and the method of payment.

5.

Often, without thinking, we do things out of habit. Some of those habits are based upon self-perceived good sense, others on some underlying fear or prejudice. We don't walk under ladders, for example.

Years ago, while working in Hong Kong, I was in the Central business district doing some banking on Des Voeux Road. In my first book, I wrote several chapters about the strange and spooky things that I experienced on this crowded, noisy, dangerous street. Here is one such true tale, noteworthy for its demonstration of unfailing Divine guidance and protection.

I emerged from the bank carrying my worn but faithful tan briefcase. I kept my briefcase close by my side carefully, as it was quite easy to get separated from possessions or loved ones in the constant stream of rushing pedestrians. The street was particularly crowded right then and folks going in both directions were bumping into my briefcase. I was becoming uneasy and glanced across the side street, noticing that the sidewalk opposite me was almost empty—by Hong Kong standards, at least. My first impulse and basic logic forcefully suggested that I dash across the street and navigate the remainder of the block in relative privacy and thus greater safety.

Suddenly that faithful voice whispered in my ear: "No, just wait!" Somewhat reluctantly, I heeded the advice, and defying what I considered to be common sense and solid logic, I plowed on straight ahead through the sidewalk crowd. At that moment, a bus passed by on the side street and stopped at the corner when it reached Des Voeux Road. There was a small crowd of pedestrians on the opposite corner waiting to cross. It was *exactly* where I would have been at that very moment, had I crossed the street at my first impulse.

The blue-and-white buses of Hong Kong Island are large, double-decker affairs. Their drivers are even more aggressive than those piloting the taxis, if you can imagine that! There's a little stick shift mounted right on the steering column and the drivers can change gears with the flick of a thumb. Often they will flip into neutral and rev up the engine while waiting impatiently at the traffic light.

I heard the engine revving and then I saw the most bizarre, unforgettable phenomenon: The front end of the huge, double-decker bus reared up into the air, with only its rear wheels remaining on the ground, not unlike a horse in a rodeo—excepting that the tare weight of this "horse" approximated twenty tons. Next came a most gruesome sight: after the front end of the bus soared high off the ground, the bus then pivoted right, *towards* the curb, before falling back to earth with a resounding crash, crushing the half-dozen folks who were waiting at the corner—on exactly the spot where I would have been! As Daniel Defoe's character "Robinson Crusoe" once wisely mused:

"How wonderfully we are delivered, when we know nothing of it. How when we are in a quandary, as we call it, a doubt or hesitation, whether to go this way, or that way, a secret hint shall direct us this way, when we intended to go that way; nay, when sense, our own inclination, and perhaps business has called to go the other way, yet a strange impression upon the mind, from we know not what springs, and by we know not what power, shall overrule us to go this way."

My good friend in Hong Kong, Melanie, called me later that evening and asked matter-of-factly: "Were you *there* today?" She had heard about that tragic bus accident on the radio. "How did you know?" I questioned, unnerved by her seeming clairvoyance.

She said that after hearing about some of my other unsettling encounters on Des Voeux Road, such as the one when Herman the German warned me of getting my wrists slit; the elderly Chinese stranger who walked out of a crowd and shook me by my goatee; my almost-departure for the nether world while not seeing hidden danger in front of me and the saga of the bouncing I-beam, she simply concluded that I was a lightning rod of sorts for bad luck on Des Voeux Road. What bouncing I-beam, you ask?

You can read more about all of these adventures in the first book of my True Tales Trilogy, *Entertaining Detours*. For now, just rejoice and celebrate with me that I received such faithful protection.

6.

Be not forgetful to entertain strangers;
for thereby some have entertained
angels unawares.

—Hebrews 13:2

For this next chapter, I will draw upon some experiences I had while in Sydney, Australia, as a young adult. And as crazy as these stories may seem, I had a witness in each instance—a sane, sober, and still-living person, who could corroborate these facts. I will just relate these stories and allow you, the reader, to make your own determination as to their possible explanation—based on whatever religion, philosophy, metaphysics or politics you may hold dear. For when it comes to the topic, some folks swear by the angels while others swear there are no such things as angels—only "coincidence" or explainable "science."

This first event happened right before midnight. I remember that because, for some reason, it was important that we got this particular batch of mail to the General Post Office in downtown Sydney for a postmark before the next day. We were probably late paying a bill or something else equally mundane. You know how it is: in hindsight, life's daily emergencies and deadlines tend to pale in their actual importance over the years.

Holding the completed mail in hand, a colleague, Chris and I headed out the back gate. This gate led to the alleyway behind Victoria Street in Potts Point. Potts Point is a euphemism for "The Neighborhood One Block away from Sodom and Gomorrah"—Sydney's famous Kings Cross—where in the evening hours, the streets' sidewalks are peopled by those of the persuasion The Kinks sang about in "*Lola*."

The alleyway dead-ended just a few feet away, where there arose a very dark, and very imposing, tall, old brick wall. Oddly enough, this wall was the far side of a nuns' convent which had somehow found the neighborhood conducive to their mission. I never asked why.

We had an old brown Bedford panel van, the kind with sliding side doors. It was a retired bread truck that we had gotten rather cheaply. Now that I think of it, this van deserves a bit more description. Firstly, there was the time while driving along one hot summer day, we decided to slide the door open for ventilation, like how all the UPS truck drivers do.

However, the door slid open a bit too far, coming completely off its rails, then becoming airborne—with me still clutching the handle. I let go just in time so as not to be sucked out into the highway along with the flying door. (There were no seat belts back in those days.)

The other odd feature of this van was its engine compartment, which opened up into the cab area via the aid of two handles that looked better suited for a bread box. Once, while driving to Sydney's Hyde Park one Sunday afternoon with my new bride in the passenger seat and a bunch of other folks sitting in the back area where loaves of bread had once been transported, this engine trap door exploded open, with bright orange flames roaring out fiercely, right between the two of us.

Somehow I had the presence of mind at that young age to immediately stop, turn off the engine, hop out (first opening that tricky sliding door), run around to the other side and pull my bride out before she herself was baked, and then run around back and open the rear door so that everyone else got out safely. Just then, a big blue city bus pulled alongside us, and the driver hopped out, brandishing his fire extinguisher and put out the blaze. Bravo! The entire event lasted only seconds. But, as a newlywed, and a young Christian, it was something you just don't quickly forget.

So, as you can see, this van did have quite the colorful history already. What had happened was the line from the fuel pump had come off the carburetor and was squirting fuel directly onto the hot engine block. The good folks at the local Napoli

Garage on Albion Street helped us replace the burnt wiring and we were good as new, which allows me to continue this tale.

As things go when you are in a terrible hurry, the battery would be dead. We were parked at the low end of the alley. Try as we might, we couldn't push the van fast enough to pop the clutch and start it that way; it was quite a challenge with just the two of us lightweights and a very heavy old van. But the mail had to get through! We prayed for help, hopefully suggesting that an angel should drop out of the sky and help us. We were out of practical ideas, obviously, and we had no AAA roadside assistance membership.

Just then, in the stillness of that dark night, we heard a loud crash behind us that made our hairs stand on end. Apparently, above that previously mentioned brick wall there was a metal roof. There were no other structures or trees above it, so there was a very short list of possibilities of what could have fallen and made such a loud thud. It turned out to be Clarence—or whatever his name was—as he didn't introduce himself.

While we stood still, transfixed, gazing up into the darkness and trying to figure out what was going on, a dark figure dressed entirely in black, including Buddy-Holly-style black eyeglasses, leapt from the roof and landed a few yards from where we stood. "Get in the van!" he ordered as he began running directly at us, at full tilt.

~ 28 ~

We were only too happy to comply, and we slammed the doors closed. "Pop it into second (gear)!" were the next and final words he spoke. Through my rearview mirror, I could see he was nearly alongside my door and at that moment he made contact with the van with another thud, this one much quieter than the last. The van roared to life, to our great relief.

Under these altered, and improved circumstances, fear immediately turned to gratitude. But there was no one around to thank! Our jump-starter vanished as quickly as he had appeared. Granted, it was dark and he was wearing black; but it was also a very long alleyway with high fences on both sides. Your call . . .

* * * * * * *

The next "mystery" took place at night also, and this time it was cold and rainy—a classic, miserable setting. The scene was by the side of the Hume Highway, partway between Sydney and Melbourne. Back then in the early '70s, life was simpler and more innocent, and hitchhiking was a fun, acceptable means of transportation—except when it was raining.

Hitchhiking was also a great way to see the countryside and meet a variety of people, the likes of which you might never otherwise encounter. Over a period of a few years while traversing much of New Zealand and Australia, I got pretty adept at the practice. Except for this particular day, when we must have had opposing cosmic headwinds. My travelling partner and I had a dozen different rides, none of them very long. The last ride dropped us off at a fork in the road, and the driver motored on home, assuring us that this was a great spot to get a ride. It wasn't.

It got darker and much colder. Vehicles passed us by and none slowed, other than just enough to take a good look at us. The rain got heavier. The unique feature of this spot where we had been let out was that there was absolutely no shelter of any kind, tree or otherwise, to be found. We tried all different styles of hitchhiking poses, but none proved any more convincing.

As it got darker and rainier, we became less visible and we had a few close calls with nearly being run over. By this time, we were fourteen hours into our day. Did I mention that we were also very hungry, thirsty and tired? "We need a miracle!" I exclaimed.

No sooner had the words fallen from my rain-soaked lips than a car screeched to a halt just ahead of us. "Hurry, get in, before you catch pneumonia!" the driver barked. (As if it were our choice to be in this predicament!) "Hungry?" he surmised. "I'll feed you, but first I have to get a little miracle," he explained.

The two of us hitchhikers silently exchanged amazed glances.

A few moments later, our rescuer stopped at a corner store, ran in and soon emerged with a small tub of "Miracle" brand margarine. I am fairly certain that he winked at us knowingly as he got in. We drove off to his place, which turned out to be a large, ramshackle car-repair garage, strewn all about with parts and tools, and sprinkled generously with oil and grease. In the midst of this filthy chaos, there stood a table and three chairs, with three dinner places already set ahead of time.

The menu included steak, vegetables and toast. The "miracle"—spread—was for the toast. My hitch-hiking buddy and I were too amazed for words. I think we were partly afraid to ask any questions, lest it all disappear just as magically as it had materialized. When our bellies were full, we became sleepy. Looking around, we saw that there was just one well-worn cot in the room.

"Ready for sleep?" our host seemed to sense. We nodded agreement and he directed us to go outside around the corner and sleep there. It was still raining. If this mess was his house, we could only imagine what the guest quarters outside around the corner must look like. But as we reluctantly, yet obediently, trudged out into the darkness, we noticed a dim light and walked toward it. It was the night-light shining in a brand new travel trailer. Yes, you guessed correctly: there were two beds already made up, with two fresh, dry towels, and a glass of water at each bedside table. We slept the sleep of the just that night.

In the morning, our mysterious host fed us breakfast. During the meal, we asked him about himself and his family. He was vague, only saying he had several sons, all around the world. He then drove us to a spot where he assured us we could easily get a good ride. (Where had we heard *that* line before?) He parked around the corner, where he could keep an eye on us. Perhaps he was a plainclothes cop? Sure enough, in under a minute, a car pulled over to pick us up.

We turned around to wave goodbye to our host, but whoever he was, he was already gone. Our new ride took us 350 miles right to the front door of our destination. Again, I'll let the conclusion be your call. Was this a visit from an angel in our time of need?

7.

. . . when thou walkest through the fire,
thou shalt not be burned, neither shall
the flame kindle upon thee.

—Isaiah 43:2

This next experience happened on a cold, windy, wintry evening in the mountains of northeast Lantau Island, near Hong Kong. You can read about my many adventures that took place during those eleven years as a missionary in south China in my first book, *Entertaining Detours*.

Local religious and cultural traditions were deeply imbedded in this region. One such aspect was "grave sweeping," whereby family members paid their respects to the departed. Fresh fruit such as mandarins or oranges were placed at the grave. Often, incense sticks were lit—as a form of prayer.

Late autumn each year brought strong winds from the north with the most unfortunate of timing: during the times of these grave-sweeping festivals. Sparks from the candles and incense lit at the ancestors' graves on the mountain tops invariably ignited the tinder-dry grasses, and entire hillsides erupted in flames within minutes. At night you could view the dramatic bright orange rings of fires circling many of Hong Kong's mountain slopes as they burned uncontrollably all night. These destructive hill fires seemed to be a yearly, unstoppable ritual.

We faced such a dire situation one night, back in the mid-1980s, when my wife and children barely escaped in time to run down the hill to stay with some neighbors, whose house was more safely surrounded by wet fields. Out of nowhere, this huge, seemingly endless wall of flames appeared at the crest of the distant mountain range to the north. At first, the danger seemed far away, but driven by fierce 50 mph winds, the flames swept down that hillside with incredible speed, so much faster than we had imagined possible!

Like the proverbial captain on the sinking ship, I had stayed behind a little longer in an effort to prepare our little property as best I could. I moved the LP gas tanks away from the kitchen to the middle of the large concrete front patio. I was very glad that the kids and I had faithfully chopped away with our garden hoe for weeks on end to clear a fire break in the thick three-foot-tall grasses surrounding the property.

Preparing for a possible emergency and actually experiencing one are two entirely different sets of emotions, however! I went to the water source—a little mountain spring up the hill that fed our water tanks—and cleared brush as best I could away from the intake pipe. Suddenly, the flames arrived on that nearby low hill, startling me. I turned quickly—too quickly—in a desperate effort to make my escape, only to hear a sickening "snap" of my ankle as my left foot caught firmly between two rocks. I was stuck!—In between a rock and a hard place.

In life-threatening moments like this, everything seems to stop, or perhaps more accurately, proceed silently, in slow motion. Suddenly all life's petty cares, desires, and concerns seem just that: petty. Your life is distilled to its most existential basics: that which is required of you in order to prevent this from becoming your last moment on earth. Neither panic nor dumb resignation to fate will satisfactorily respond to such a challenge. I could only manage a one-word prayer for help, "Jesus!"

Somehow, a combination of the angels, good karma and an adrenaline-induced boost of clear thinking extricated me out of that predicament, and I finally escaped to safety. As I stumbled down the dark path, I asked for the Lord's protection of our property and possessions we had left behind.

For he shall give his angels charge over thee, to keep thee in all thy ways. They shall bear thee up in their hands, lest thou dash thy foot against a stone. —Psalm 91:11-12

The intense flames roared and popped all night long.

The next morning, when all the flames had died down, I cautiously crept back up the hill, with still-smoking bushes on both sides of the pathway. I was half-hopeful, and half-sick with fear over what I imagined would be a sight of total devastation. The entire hillside of the valley was blackened and all that tall grass and thick shrubbery had been reduced to gray, powdery ash!

Suddenly, as I rounded a corner in the path, I could make out what appeared to be an acre of bright *green* in the midst of all those blackened hillsides— it was our home! Our firebreaks had held! Not one blade of grass on that acre of ours had burned. The water source was not damaged, and water still faithfully flowed from the spring, out of the rocky, now-barren hillside. Even the garden hoe which I had hastily thrown down in my escape was left completely unscathed by the flames, outlined in green in the midst of that blackened hillside.

We happily and gratefully moved back into our home later that day! Later, the spring rains came and restored the hillsides to their former verdant splendor.

8.

Those that walk in pride he is able to abase.

—*Daniel 4:37*

Spiritual pride is a rather nebulous concept, but once in a while it surfaces in graphic fashion. For the most part, preaching the Gospel is a humbling experience. Occasionally, some individual attempts to steal the spotlight from its Divine owner, often with comic, or tragic, consequences.

This first account falls more towards the comic end of the spectrum. In Canberra, Australia's capital city, a group of us young lay preachers were having moderate success sharing the Good News with local university students. This news caught the ear of a local Pentecostal preacher we had met. We had considered it odd that Pastor Smith's day job was at the local abattoir. It seemed ironic that someone patterning his spiritual efforts after that of the Great Shepherd would work 9 to 5 Monday through Friday slaughtering sheep.

Pastor Smith asked for a sit-down with us to hear our strategies, so as to glean tips on how he might improve his own local outreach efforts. At one point, the discussion became rather heated when we pointed out to him that proselytizing was perhaps more effective when done on a full-time basis, as was the case with the early disciples two millennia ago. He became rather agitated, arguing strenuously that such talk was nonsense, and outdated.

As we persisted with our line of argument, offering Scriptures from the Book of Acts of the Apostles as evidence, Pastor Smith boiled over in rage. From my experience, such rage usually masks a futile attempt to resist the conviction of the Holy Spirit. His face now beet red, the angry man argued forcefully, so forcefully in fact that two of the buttons from his white long-sleeved shirt popped off and sailed clear across the room, and in the process exposed his very broad, hairy chest. We excused ourselves at that point and left. (Someone later remarked about being reminded of the warning from Matthew 7:15 at that moment, *Beware of false prophets, which come to you in sheep's clothing, but inwardly they are ravening wolves.*)

Pastor Smith was very proud of the van he drove around while preaching. He was even prouder of the Hawaiian-style slide guitar he loved to play, which he kept inside the van. Pastor Smith was not what you would call an accomplished musician by any means, but that did not deter him. He would play away on that instrument whether the moment was appropriate or not, just whenever the mood struck him. It was like the antics of a spoiled child.

It was his plan that particular weekend to have a spectacularly successful revival at a local park, and thereby show us that his weekend efforts were not to be sneezed at, that he could be just as successful, if not more so, than we had been. We had no further desire to argue with him, nor compete with him, and so we simply committed the matter to God.

We arrived to watch how things would turn out for him. It was a pretty sunny day, and the grassy slope seemed exceptionally green. The operative word here is "slope." Pastor Smith parked his van, loaded with his precious electric slide guitar at the top of the slope and strutted off to chat with some folks prior to getting underway with the main events. We glanced over at the van, only to behold it slowly and silently, in bizarre fashion, rolling down the slope, gaining momentum as it went along.

Out of the corner of his eye, Pastor Smith caught sight of what was happening and rushed back in an attempt to rescue the situation. Perhaps in his excited haste he had forgotten to put the parking brake on fully. In any event, his stubby legs were not fast enough to catch up with the van which was now hurtling toward the precipice at the end of that grassy, green field. Over the edge flew the van, with the electric slide guitar, the amplifier, the cords, the Gospel tracts, and whatever else was inside the doomed vehicle.

We never heard any more from Pastor Smith, or from his electric Hawaiian-style slide guitar from that day hence . . .

* * * * * * *

This next story is harder for me to relate. It is an amazing story, and I remember the details vividly. I'm hesitant only because I don't want to portray myself as being something special. I was just in the right place at the right time.

This experience took place in Sydney's southern suburbs. We had a young worker who was very charming—handsome, charismatic, talented and witty. The danger when witnessing the Gospel is the temptation to draw attention, and/or credit to oneself, rather than to the original Author of that Good News. Ralph—as we'll call him for the purposes of this lesson—had quite the following of young ladies who found the charming lad to be rather irresistible.

I counseled Ralph to be aware of the effect all this adulation was having upon his motivation and judgement. He dismissed my advice as being overly serious and out of touch. Soon he won the attention of an attractive young lady attending the University of Sydney. Her father was chief of police in an affluent neighborhood. She visited for Bible studies, but her interactions with Ralph became more like dating. We usually encouraged our mission workers to travel two-by-two, for safety and to provide opportunity for counsel.

Ralph ignored our standing policy and headed out clandestinely one afternoon to spend the day at the beach with his pretty new recruit. Around sunset I received a frantic call. Ralph was in trouble. All of the swagger was gone from his voice. Something was very wrong. The girl was unconscious and was not breathing. In his desperation, Ralph confessed that they'd been drinking, and then had sex together. Additionally, they'd been out in the hot sun for hours and she was now undoubtedly dehydrated as well.

I'd met this girl's father previously on several occasions. He was a reasonable man, but also a concerned parent. He had quizzed me extensively on our Biblical beliefs until he was satisfied that we were not "Hare Krishna or something like that." I think what tipped the scales in our favor was when I agreed to have a beer with him, whereupon he then considered me a "normal" Aussie.

He was very firm and quite accustomed to having his orders followed. As I hung up from Ralph's call, I could hardly imagine myself having to face the girl's father with this terrible news. I was certain there would be dire consequences for Ralph and perhaps for our outreach as well.

When I arrived at the scene, the young lady was indeed quite lifeless. I began to pray for all I was worth! In that stressful moment, I suddenly heard the authoritative—yet calming—voice of the Word of God in my heart:

These signs shall follow them that believe in me: In my name . . . they shall lay hands on the sick, and they shall recover.

—Mark 16:17-18.

While it was quite obvious that this young lady was more than just *sick*, I felt quite certain that I had received very specific instructions in answer to my prayer. As I laid hands upon her, I was fully aware that any Divine answer would be as a result of mercy, and not from any earned merit. Ralph stood by, silent and pale, hardly breathing himself. When I finished praying, concluding, "In Jesus name," I heard the most wonderful sound: The young woman took a deep breath, the color returned to her face, and she sat up, quite naturally, as if nothing had happened.

Ralph no longer chided me about being an old fuddy-duddy. He was silent for quite some time. I sensed he was fully aware that he had barely missed a lightning bolt, as it were. His massive ego had suffered a serious setback.

A few weeks later, he soon lost interest and went his own way, like a restless moth seeking a new flame.

2.

And the peace of God, which passeth all understanding, shall keep your hearts and minds through Christ Jesus.

—Philippians 4:7

Sometimes, with certain endeavors, the harder you try, the less success you seem to have. This is the scenario where frustration naturally sets in. It would appear that the Law of Diminishing Returns is ruling your life. To the Creator, this is nothing more than another opportunity to amaze and nurture the believer.

I had been a full-time Christian missionary for about three years at this point in time. I was living in Sydney, Australia, where we had been blessed with a number of new converts who were all desirous of further Bible training. Our outreach was conducted where there was the most need: in the busy, noisy, dangerous inner city. A more peaceful environment would be conducive to concentrated studies.

My supervisor was leaving for an extended mission trip to Indonesia. The task would fall to me to locate the proper training facility. "Don't let these folks down! They are counting on you!" were his parting words. I felt an enormous, uninvited weight of responsibility settling upon my shoulders. And then he was off on his flight.

I tried all avenues I could think of: newspapers, real estate agents, magazines, chambers of commerce. Mind you, this was long before the days of the internet, if you can imagine that. This story might not have happened in recent times. It would not seem that difficult to search for properties, using a search engine. Our "search engine" at the time was an old, blue Nissan minivan.

A few teams of volunteers headed out, looking for a suitable property, fanning out to all compass points. None of the teams had anything promising to report when they returned. Meanwhile, the calendar pages marched on inexorably. I started thinking about the verse in Ezekiel chapter 33 about "their blood being upon your (my) hand." I was quite desperate, to say the least. I was driven to my knees, fortunately.

"God, I just don't understand! We are trying so hard! This is so important! We are all praying! Why can't we find what we need?" I inquired. The answer I received came as a verse of Scripture, spoken to my heart, after which I felt tremendously relieved.

The peace of God, which passes all understanding, shall keep your hearts and minds through Christ Jesus.

The words went directly from the printed page into my soul. I stopped worrying. We took a break from our searching and resumed normal life.

A couple of friends were vacationing in the Blue Mountains, and had stopped for a drink at a local pub in Springwood, at the foothills of their journey. They got to chatting with someone who mentioned there was an old farmhouse needing some tender loving care. They went to take a look, and then phoned me. "We found something that might be what you are looking for. Believe it or not, there is a verse of Scripture on a framed needlework piece over the mantle of the living room fireplace," they reported.

"Don't tell me!" I interrupted. "That verse is 'The peace of God, which passes all understanding, shall keep your hearts and minds through Christ Jesus,' right?"

The phone went silent for a moment and then the caller exclaimed. "How did you know?"

I had no doubt as to which verse was displayed on that wall, one hundred kilometers away. I did not need to see it to know that. I also had no doubt that this was indeed the place we were meant to have. I did not need to see it to confirm the discovery myself. There was also no way that any of us could claim that our collective wisdom, or our combined efforts had located the correct piece of real estate.

As it turned out, we could not have found a place more suitable to our needs. We couldn't have asked for a more helpful, accommodating landlord. The rental price was minimal. Facilities were limitless. The surroundings were awe-inspiring. The property served us well for many years. In time, we invited other church groups to hold their retreats in this idyllic spot.

Once our hearts were at peace, God was able to work on our behalf. There are 31,102 verses in the Bible. If you contend that this experience was pure coincidence, you must at least admit that the odds were rather long.

10.

And I will bless them that bless thee, and curse him that curseth thee.

—Genesis 12:3

I hesitate to tell this story. It is entirely true. It testifies to the power of prayer. It will also offend some folks' sense of propriety. This event took place in Japan three decades ago, in a remote rural fishing town. There some fellow missionaries had set up a boarding school for the children of missionaries at a facility loaned to us by a wealthy local businessman.

The property had been in a state of disuse and thus disrepair for some time. We set about to restore the buildings and grounds. Volunteer labor transformed the property into a pleasant, attractive setting. A park was built, and was made available to the public for their use at no charge.

As the facility was enhanced and expanded, teachers were recruited. Additional students arrived until full capacity was reached. There was a waiting list for new students. Classes were taught in English and

Japanese. State-of-the-art audio and video studios were added. Our gardener exchanged flowers and local produce with the other farmers in the area. People came from faraway Tokyo and beyond to tour the facility, garnering ideas for their own educational programs. All seemed to be going well.

Then one day, a middle-aged local woman took it upon herself to launch a vile campaign against our project. Whether she took exception to our being Christians who had a growing number of Japanese adherents, or whether she just took exception to our being foreigners, or both, was not entirely clear. What was clear was her intention to smear our good name, in an effort to have us driven from the area.

Repeated invitations to meet with her, to discuss her grievances, were rebuffed. Instead, she went to all the local neighbors and told the most salacious stories about us. According to her, we were the Japanese branch of the Charles Manson killers. We were pure evil. The more sensational of the local newspapers listened to her, as her story would help sell papers to any readers who were looking for a juicy story about these foreigners.

Much time, money and effort had been invested in our boarding school project over the years. Much good had been accomplished. Other than not being from around there, we had not committed any crimes. The decision had to be made whether or not to pack up and leave, as this woman's crusade was making it quite impossible for our operations to continue.

Before any extensive plans to evacuate the facilities were set in motion, it was decided to have a prayer meeting. All concerned were invited to attend. The purpose of the meeting was to pray for the woman in question. Whereas, we ourselves had been unable to meet or influence this woman's thoughts and intents, perhaps Divine intervention could be called upon to conciliate on our behalf.

Fervent and sincere prayers were expressed. We asked for God's merciful intervention. If it were at all possible, we petitioned, perhaps this person could have a change of heart. In that way, we could carry on the beneficial work we were doing. When everyone who wished had had an opportunity to pray, we concluded our meeting, hopeful of positive results. Everyone went home for the night.

Within a couple days, there was a buzz of informal news spreading around the otherwise quiet country-side. One of the neighbors had gone by to visit this woman at her home. She was an energetic, active woman and her absence had been quickly noticed. The local authorities were called to her home. The woman had been found in her bed, unresponsive. It was determined that she had died of a heart attack the previous day.

This was not the answer to prayer we had expected and it was certainly not an occasion to rejoice. We were, nevertheless, in respectful awe of what had just transpired. The woman's heart had indeed been changed, but in a much more dramatic, permanent way than we had envisioned when we had prayed. It was certainly not a time for gloating, lest a similar misfortune befall any of us. (Proverbs 24:17-18)

* * * * * *

This story is not meant to encourage others to pray for, or hope for, such drastic results. It is meant to serve as a sober reminder that we have no control over precisely how the Creator chooses to answer our prayers.

It is a fearful thing to fall into the hands
of the living God.
—Hebrews 10:31

And now, Lord, behold their threatenings; and grant unto thy servants, that with all boldness they may speak thy word, By stretching forth thine hand to heal; and that signs and wonders may be done by the name of thy holy child, Jesus. And when they had prayed, the place was shaken where they were assembled together; and they were all filled with the Holy Ghost, and they spake the word of God with boldness.

—Acts 4:29-31

11.

He keepeth all his bones: not one of
them is broken.

—Psalm 34:20

L et's now move on to a somewhat lighter note. Many of my readers are parents. You are fully aware of the many pitfalls along the road to successful parenting. No matter how hard you try to protect your child from harm, danger seems to lurk around every corner. Believing parents have found that a daily prayer of protection goes a long ways. When we can't be everywhere, guardian angels sometimes step in and save the day.

I need to tell you about a horse incident. This event happened when my first son was still just a toddler, some four decades ago, when we lived in Sydney, Australia. My parents came for a visit one Christmas and we took them around to see the various grandparent-friendly venues in Sydney, such as the Taronga Park Zoo.

I had spotted a nature reserve/petting zoo marked on the map way out in the western suburbs and felt we could give that a try. That turned out to be a mistake. The owners had apparently long since given up trying to maintain any semblance of a respectable establishment, but they were still collecting admission. It had been a long drive to get there and now that we were there, we reluctantly paid up and went in, searching for whatever fun and adventure we could find.

The animals did not look like they had had any fun for quite some time, and not that much food either. James, my number one son, was all of about two years old at this point and full of energy, with the occasional mishap. He was very excited to see a horse and was quite impatient with our slow pace. He squirmed and broke away from our grip and went charging after an old, gray sway-back plow horse grazing in the distance on the few remaining blades of grass.

My calls to James to wait up for us went unheeded. So we had no choice but to chase after him, trying to get to James before he could get to the back of that horse. Somehow his little legs outran us all, and we resorted to frantically yelling after him to stop.

Then it happened. That old cantankerous horse was in no mood to entertain strangers, let alone an energetic little ankle-biter. So he did what horses do in such situations: he reared back and kicked for all he was worth, and unfortunately, right on target. The horse's left hind foot connected squarely with James, who came hurtling back towards us, flying through the air and then landing with a loud *thud* in a heap on the ground ahead of us.

There was only time for a quick, desperate prayer to be uttered while my son was airborne. Soon, the gathering of horrified adults caught up to the scene of the accident. My wife was quick to point out that this calamity was entirely my fault, for picking this miserable park. She ordered me to be the one to go and check on our son's condition.

Meanwhile, everyone else held their breath. With a heavy heart, I set out with shaky legs to collect my firstborn. I was expecting a rather gruesome scene, with at least several broken bones. I wasn't sure if he was even conscious. The horse's kick had been so vicious, and my son was so tiny.

When little James saw me bend down to look at him, he promptly broke out into gleeful giggles. I exhaled, being somewhat relieved that he seemed in good spirits. I then examined him, searching to find what must be a huge imprint from the horse's hoof in his little torso, but there was none!

I asked my new little rodeo clown where that nasty horse had kicked him, and he proudly pointed to his left knee. I could find no mark or swelling at all. He ran off to his mother, excited to tell her all about his big adventure. To this day, my left knee aches when the weather changes . . .

12.

Because thou hast made the Lord, which is my refuge,
even the most High, thy habitation;
There shall no evil befall thee, neither shall any
plague come nigh thy dwelling.

—Psalm 91: 9-10

We are neither omnipresent nor omniscient. Regardless of how careful we may try to be, and how well-meaning our intentions, we are still unable to foresee every possibility and prevent every tragic accident. Fortunately, we have an advocate, a supreme Entity, who is omnipotent.

In this chapter, I will relate two stories of situations regarding properties we were renting, where a faulty heating system could easily have cost the lives of my entire family. Both experiences involved dangerous situations that we were totally unaware of. Both of these episodes have happy endings, no thanks to me.

Years ago, we rented a cute, little wood-frame house in a working class suburb of Sydney, Australia. The house came with a fireplace. This was a plus in the chilly southern hemisphere winter months of July and August, as the houses there were not centrally heated. So in we moved, my wife and our two little ones, James and Suzy.

Before moving into a house, some critical details you might not consider—unless you are a contractor, which I wasn't—might include the straightness of the chimney. It turns out, the chimney's straightness is very important. When we first moved in, I went all around the house and yard, checking things out. It was fun discovering the charms of a new home. I did look to see if there was a chimney before we began using the fireplace, and sure enough, there it was, sticking up straight out of the roof, and seemingly in great condition. This was a novice's assessment, obviously.

We enjoyed our cozy little fires for quite a few winter days in that living room. On one particular evening before closing the living room door and going into the dining room for supper, I glanced up at the ceiling after I turned out the light. *Odd,* I thought to myself, *someone left the light on in the attic!* I could see light coming through the narrow cracks in the old-style wooden ceiling. Then three thoughts quickly dawned on me in rapid succession: firstly, that there was no attic and secondly, that there was no lighting up there. The third thought crashed and stopped my heart momentarily: *if it was not an electric light up in the attic, then the "light" I saw was instead actually the bright flames from a blazing fire!*

We quickly got the kids safely outside into the big back yard and called the local fire department. Meanwhile, an anonymous "passerby" spotted the smoke and flames escaping from our roof, grabbed a neighbor's garden hose and somehow got up on the roof and began dousing the flames. His quick action kept the fire's damage to a minimum. The mystery volunteer fire-fighter disappeared without a trace.

We had to leave our happy home and stay with friends for a month or so while the restoration work was done. The postmortem on the fiery disaster revealed that the chimney that led up from the fireplace *stopped* at the floor of the attic. Closer examination revealed that the chimney visible from the exterior was about twelve inches offset from the current fireplace's chimney. Either there had been some strange remodeling done over the years, or the house had suffered a weird tectonic plate shift.

This meant that all of those weeks that we had been happily burning a cozy fire in that little fireplace, we were blissfully ignorant that hot little embers were rising up that truncated chimney and settling on top of the wooden ceiling above our heads. Eventually, a critical mass of hot embers accumulated, sufficient to encourage the wooden planks to ignite. Thus the bright "light" I saw in the attic that fateful evening.

We bought a little electric room heater after that.

* * * * *

Now let's spin the globe and move your attention 8,000 miles northeast. About two decades later, and now raising my second family of six children (you are correct: yes, twelve wonderful children in all!), I had just rented a 100-year-old farmhouse in rural Texas. The quaint old property had a huge propane tank outside, feeding its crucial fuel to the three ancient rickety heaters via an underground metal pipe. Our house had pier-and-beam foundation construction that was typically used in those days, being most suitable for the shifting prairie soils of East Texas. Thus, there was a small crawl space under the floorboards for access to the plumbing.

We were fresh arrivals from big city living, but we had already learned about the smell of a skunk. We thought the lingering odor near the back door must have been from a skunk that had lived under the house during the years while the house sat vacant. However, the odor actually signaled a more sinister problem.

When we arrived at our new rent home, as retired missionaries, we were far from wealthy. It was a considerable investment to have that big propane tank refilled. It was a particularly cold winter for Texas that year and the old yet-to-be-upgraded windows were very drafty, so we ran those heaters non-stop. Still, it seemed that propane tank ran out way too soon and yet the "skunk" smell seemed stronger than ever. These old heaters were the kind you light with a match.

Before this next tale, I need to offer some historical background: Back on March 18th 1937, 300 school children in New London, Texas perished when the pent-up leaking—and then-odorless—natural gas exploded, literally blowing the roof off the school, leveling the building, and creating a blast felt by residents forty miles away. Some students and teachers miraculously survived the immense explosion, one of those being Mrs. Judy Arnold.

I had the pleasure to meet Judy, who was the mother of Penny Arnold, the businesswoman who had just hired me to help run her business, now some sixty years after that natural gas disaster. When Judy talked to me about her incredible experience, I then learned about *malodorants*, which are the additives mixed in with the otherwise naturally-scentless natural gas to give it that distinctive skunky smell. In that way, there would never again be a disaster, the likes of New London.

Unbeknownst to me at the time, malororants was what I had actually smelled under my back porch. This would have explained why the huge propane tank emptied so quickly. But this mystery would go unsolved for a year. By the next winter, we had managed to save enough money to pay for plumbers to install new gas lines and hook us up to the city gas supply. The old propane tank was hauled away, but the old underground vestigial iron pipes remained.

The following year our boys—Mikael, Martin and Richard—and I began digging some of that shifting sand out from under the living room floor where it had slithered in from the hillside to the south. While digging away, I came across a length of the very old and by now, very rusty pipe that once had fed the propane to the heater in the living room.

I dug down into the sandy ground until I could uncover the pipe. Upon removing it, I found I only had half a pipe in my hand, so to speak: The entire bottom half of the pipe for a foot-long section was completely corroded away! The shifting sands in which that gas pipe had been buried had apparently acted as a safety wrap of sorts. The sand kept the gas trapped underground, but allowed some of the malodorant to rise, which was that "skunk" smell that had persisted.

Furthermore, where this gap in the pipe occurred was directly under the floor boards of the room where I had been cluelessly lighting matches all that first winter when starting that heater. The flame from my matches could not have been more than eighteen inches from that leaking gas pipe below!

I froze in place as the significance of this discovery slowly reached deep inside me. We had somehow been spared a similar fate to those in New London some six decades prior. "Hallelujah!" was all I could shout out spontaneously, in that confined crawl space under our house that day. Words sometimes fail when one is confronted with the awesome fact that your family had been mercifully spared a certain death, once again.

13.

Lo, children are an heritage of the Lord; and the fruit of the womb is his reward.

—Psalm 127:3

Parenthood is a tremendous blessing, as well as an extremely serious responsibility. The new life emerges into this hostile world with none of its own defenses yet in place. The role of the parents is to provide that nurture and protection as best they can, with help from above.

The duty of the parent can be frustrating and frightening, as well as rewarding and wonderful. Childhood crises should drive the believer often to prayer, for guidance and strength. I can't imagine raising children without a belief that a force greater than myself is in control.

Birth defects, childhood illnesses, and accidents are just some of the obstacles along the road to the successful development of a new human being. In this chapter, I will reflect on a few of the challenges that I faced as a parent when encountering some of these obstacles, with the intention of demonstrating the awesome power of my Creator.

The things which are impossible with
men are possible with God.
—Luke 18:27

My first son, James, weighed in at only 2.2 kilograms at birth, or just under five pounds. The doctors recommended that we keep him in the hospital for weeks. My wife and I made the decision to take him home with us, despite the chorus of dire warnings of the horrible consequences of our action. James did just fine. He seemed perpetually hungry, and nursed every two hours for about the first year of his life, but he grew to be a fine, strong, intelligent man. Along the way, there were many challenges.

The first big challenge came when James learned to crawl. He could accelerate quite rapidly when he was focused on a target. His target that day was his mom's cup of hot tea. Before she had a chance to move it, he was upon it, and stuck his chubby little hand into the boiling hot water. He screamed and cried miserably in pain.

Very fortunately, there was a nurse visiting at the time. She immediately tended to the little fellow. She had had advanced training in burn treatment, and knew to wrap a special bubbled-gauze bandage between our baby's little fingers, so as to prevent the fingers from growing together when healing.

Perhaps even more amazing, was the fact that this nurse had just arrived from Perth, Australia, some 2,500 miles away. This woman was formerly a practicing witch, who had converted to Christianity quite recently. The timing of all these events seems more than just mere coincidence. James healed up perfectly.

When Suzy was born in Brisbane, she weighed in at eight pounds. We placed our newborn daughter in her bed, and being ourselves quite exhausted, we immediately fell sound asleep. When I awoke, it was morning. I had slept for eight hours. Having become accustomed to our first child waking every two hours, I was concerned and rushed to Suzy's bedside, fearing the worst. But there she was, sleeping quite peacefully. Our little girl slept through every night, and her tired parents caught up on eighteen months of broken sleep.

A year later, a dark cloud came over her sunny days. A deep purple boil appeared suddenly on her tiny neck and grew large and hard. Our lively daughter was listless and nearly comatose as I held her in my arms on the way to the hospital. I remained on vigil in the park outside, keeping James occupied while his mom was with Suzy in the surgery room.

After a while, a nurse beckoned us, telling us it was time for us to come in. I was hesitant, uncertain of what awaited us. Suddenly, I heard the heartening sound of familiar laughter. The surgeon explained to us that as soon as he had lanced open her neck, the pent-up infection exploded across the room. Once the pressure was released, Suzy was her happy and healthy self once more. The dark clouds departed.

A couple years later when Suzy's new sister, Joanne, was born, the doctor grimly informed us that our baby had a birth defect in her hip, which would prevent her from being able to walk. We were naturally quite shocked, and devastated. When the doctor left, the head nurse gathered us close and told us not to worry.

She had often seen this "click in the hip"—as she called it—and knew of a simple remedy. She told us to use a double diaper for the first year. These were still the days of cloth diapers. The second diaper was to help spread the hips enough so they could set and grow properly. A year later, Joanne was soon running around after her brother and sister. Now she is a lovely, energetic mother of three, who spent ten years walking just fine, all over Nigeria, as a missionary.

A decade later when Martin was born in Vienna, Austria, he emerged looking like a tiny, bug-eyed mouse. He was quite tiny at birth, as was James. Martin had somehow survived having the umbilical cord wrapped around his neck *three* times, a medical rarity. Once the doctor managed to untangle the little fellow, he progressed just fine.

A year and a half later, we were visiting a museum in a nearby castle. Martin went charging ahead of me, not unlike James had done long ago, chasing after that mean horse. Martin was giggling, thrilled with his new freedom, since learning to propel himself. He was also headed right for disaster. He was tiny enough that he could run under the display tables.

The tables were made with heavy metal braces, which ran along the floor between the four legs of the table. Martin's little feet caught the brace at the front of the table, and tripping, he went airborne. His trajectory was such that his forehead would land on the brace at the opposite side of the table. I was running after him, but I would be too late to protect him. I barely had time to send up a quick prayer for protection before I heard the sickening *thud* as his head landed and bounced. I was horrified, certain that I was about to find a huge gash in his skull.

Then I heard that wonderful sound that instantly eradicates parents' worst fears, the sound of their child laughing. Some angel obviously had gotten between Martin and that heavy metal cross brace to cushion his impact. He did not even have a scratch on him, and I was soon able to breathe once again.

Over the years, Martin survived other bumps on the head and various mishaps. In spite of the water buffaloes, typhoons, deadly snakes, fires, vehicle accidents, and epidemics, all twelve children eventually arrived at their adulthood in great shape, ready to face the world, and one day become parents themselves . . .

14.

*Call unto me, and I will answer thee, and shew thee
great and mighty things,
which thou knowest (understand) not.*

—*Jeremiah 33:3*

There was a storm in the media over the comments that Pope Francis allegedly made to a crowd of some 33,000 people in Rome on June 25th, 2017. It is reported that the Pope warned his listeners that "having a personal relationship with Jesus is dangerous and very harmful." The Catholic faithful was lectured that "a personal, direct, immediate relationship with Jesus Christ" must be avoided at all costs. Apparently, the matter of communicating with the Almighty is best left to the religious professionals.

Perhaps the Pontiff misspoke. Perhaps his words have been taken out of context. I will leave that up to the reader to decide. Another famous speech was recorded 2,000 years ago. Jesus Christ told those listening that day, "I am the way and the truth and the life. No one comes to the Father except through Me." (John 14:6) No mention was made then as to the need for intermediaries. A further promise was made that ". . . him that cometh to me I will in no wise cast out." (John 6:37) This later statement seems to negate any fear that approaching God directly would be dangerous for those who attempt to do so.

I suppose it could be argued that there is merit in the Pope's cautionary words. History is replete with cases of individuals and armies that have done unspeakable evil to their fellow man, all the while claiming "God told me to do it." Whether for a serial killer or for the commander of nation, such a carte-blanche fiat is indeed dangerous and harmful.

Theology is much like politics in some ways: their teachings serve to maintain the status quo. No one likes losing their job, be they senator or priest. Ideologies help shield such folks from the vagaries of normal life. I can only relate what I have personally experienced, and have no desire to impose my beliefs or preferences upon the reader.

When I first traveled to the mission field in the South Pacific, my initial stop was Auckland, New Zealand. The agency arranging my trip sent a letter ahead to a doctor and his wife there, who would be my temporary host. They were to meet me at the airport. Having committed myself to the calling to be a missionary, I did not see the need for a return ticket. I had no plan for looking back.

My flight from Chicago to Auckland in a 707 jet, before the days of Jumbo 747s, was a 27-hour ordeal, hopping to Honolulu and next to Samoa and then Fiji en route. It was well after midnight the next day when I passed through New Zealand customs and immigrations and into the tiny arrival hall. There was no one there to greet me.

I was struck with a flood of self-doubt. Perhaps I had made a wrong decision; perhaps I had been too hasty. I had not quite reached my 21st birthday at this point, and had never flown more than 200 miles before. I was certainly out of my depth. I was 8,000 miles from home, and knew no one in this country.

I went to the phone book and looked up the doctor's name in the directory. It was not listed there. Next I called the operator and asked if she might be able to check for the number. Her efforts came up empty as well. I thanked the operator for her time, and hung up. I wandered around the now nearly deserted terminal, trying desperately to come up with a plan. At present, I was homeless.

I prayed. I acknowledged my pride and my ambition and my lack of knowledge and experience. I asked for mercy to override my errors in judgement. And I asked for guidance. Hoping for something profound and encouraging, I received a message in my mind of just two words: "New listings."

This made even less sense to me than the plight I was already in. I had only one acquaintance in New Zealand so far, that being the telephone operator. So I called her back.

"May I help you?" she answered.

"New Listings," I blurted out.

"I beg your pardon, what number are you calling?"

"It's me again, trying to reach Dr. Phillips. Does 'new listings' mean anything to you? Those words just came to me when I was praying," I explained.

"Why yes, of course! New Listings is a term we have for recently-installed phones, not yet listed in either the printed phone directories nor on our central records. Let me check," the operator offered helpfully.

Soon I was on the phone with a very sleepy Mrs. Phillips at the other end. After apologizing for waking her, I introduced myself and explained my situation. They had not yet received the letter with details of my arrival, but they were happy I had made it safely, nonetheless, she explained.

"Hurry now and you might be able to catch the last bus into the city," Mrs. Phillips instructed.

The final bus leaving the airport for the long drive to the city was just beginning to pull away from the curb as I rushed to hop aboard. It would be seven hours before the next bus in the morning.

An hour or so later after catching a cab from the bus terminal to the Phillips' home, I stood at their front door, breathless and excited. The next day, the letter that had traveled 8,000 miles from The States came in the mail, announcing my impending arrival.

15.

The beasts of the field shall be at peace with thee.

—*Job 5:23*

There were many inherent dangers to living in various Third World countries, including wild animals. Over the years I've encountered wild boars, cobras, bamboo pit vipers, scorpions, spiders that were the size of your hand, and centipedes that were as long as a man's foot, and an eighteen-foot-long King Cobra.

In China, I encountered some of the most vicious, disease-ridden and downright ugly dogs imaginable, except for one, who adopted me and my young children. They named him "Happy Ending."

In life, not all endings are happy. Some are. The ending to the path in peaceful Tung Hang Mei Valley on Lantau Island led to our happy little slice of paradise, tucked around the mountains and across the West Lamma Channel portion of the South China Sea, far away from the noisy concrete jungle of the Hong Kong "mainland." The ending—of our dog's tail—was always wagging with happiness.

It was a long and winding footpath that led up from the MuiWo ferry pier to our gated home in the mountain valley. If you are well-conditioned, it takes a half hour to walk up the hilly path.   Downhill on bicycle is only ten minutes if there is no "traffic"— like a cartload of pigs on their way to market, or a huge spider web stretched across the path.

During the approximately 363 days of the year when it is humid in Hong Kong, it was a relief at the half-way point up our path to reach the "bus stop" for a break before ascending the steepest part of the journey.   We humorously called it the "bus stop" because there were no buses or cars of any type; there were only people, bicycles, and pushcarts on this path.

The "bus stop" was a sturdy concrete structure with benches under its welcoming shade. Right next to the bus stop was a ramshackle dwelling where a most unpleasant gentleman lived. From the yellow coloring of his eyes, it seemed he lived mostly on a liquid diet of a near-fatal brew of some vile concoction. His place was filthy and a total mess.

That was, except for this gorgeous copper-haired little dog with the waggiest white-tipped tail you have ever seen. The dog seemed greatly cheered every time he saw us. His tail wagged furiously when he spotted us! The dear creature must have sensed a touch of kindness that was otherwise lacking in his life. His owner did not seem to be the personality you would want working at an animal shelter, for example.

One day, the kids excitedly noticed that there was a cute dog at our gate happily wagging its tail. Thus they dubbed him "Happy Ending." He was trailing a leash of sorts and had obviously broken free and followed our scent up the mile-long stretch from the "bus stop." I sadly told the kids that the dog had an owner, and I walked the poor dog back to that salty character, albeit not without serious misgivings. I did have respect for property rights, such as they were; and I was a guest in this country, a "foreign devil" at that. So I did what I thought was proper. The next day, the same dog was happily at our gate again. Again I returned the dog to its disagreeable owner, who simply grunted.

That dog and I made that pilgrimage up and down that steep path countless times, each time with a thicker and heavier leash attached which Happy Ending had somehow managed to break. It seemed that Happy Ending was very *un*happy with his master. I know you can imagine hearing my children's voices in the background "can we keep him, Daddy?!" One of those thankless chores of a parent is trying to convincingly explain to them why they couldn't, when I wasn't all that convinced myself.

As they say, "don't leave school until the bell rings." We had a shiny little bicycle bell attached to our gate so arriving visitors could signal us. One morning the bell rang.   It was Happy Ending, carried by his grumpy, disheveled owner.   When we opened the gate, he handed the dog to us without a word and walked off. I guess he decided it was too expensive and bothersome to keep buying stouter leashes to restrain his dog. The kids were ecstatic.

Happy Ending was so beautiful and so very happy. We all had lots of fun chasing each other around the yard and being amused by how fast and furiously Happy Ending could wag that tail of his! He slept right outside the front double doors, guarding his new home at night and waiting for us to wake up and play with him each day.

Every day we seemed to have a different snake pass through our yard, often a new variety. Then, the fateful night came when a cobra slithered into our front yard and faithful Happy Ending barked furiously to warn us before bravely attacking the intruder. Alas, the cobra prevailed. Happy Ending died that night defending his little family. We found him the next morning lying on the front patio under the big shade tree, stiff as a board, the early sunlight reflecting off his copper coat for the last time.

* * * * * *

Years later, I was in Mexico, where it is also prudent to avoid any loose dogs. I lived in Chipinque, which was a lovely neighborhood perched in the verdant cool shade of the Sierra Madres, high above the sweltering hot and dusty city of Monterrey far below. The property we rented came with a "free" dog. "Lady" was a beautiful, ghost-silver Great Dane who had been horribly mistreated, and finally abandoned. We kept her and nursed her back to health and gradually calmed her fears.

One evening, I went out to feed Lady. It was dark, but I knew the pathway around the side of the house well, and did not bother to turn on the outside light. Suddenly, I sensed an unusual presence and before I could react, a very large male Rottweiler appeared directly in front of me. He jumped up and laid one huge paw on my left shoulder, followed by the other equally large paw on my right shoulder.

The dog and I were now looking eye to eye. Over the years of encountering unfriendly dogs in the various hamlets I passed while hiking the mountains of Lantau Island, I'd learned not to show fear. So I did my best to remain calm. The Rottweiler's massive jaw was just an inch from my nose and I could feel his hot breath. I spoke softly and slowly. "Nice dog. You sure are a handsome dog. You are very strong. I bet you would like someone to scratch you."

I had read somewhere that when talking to a dog, it's best to communicate while thinking of images. I was trying to imagine a nice, calm dog rolling over so I could scratch his belly. Instead, the Rottweiler took my left forearm in his mouth and closed down ever so slightly. I could sense the immense power of his jaws, but felt no pain. He then released his grip, and licked my arm. We became best friends. I dubbed him "Rocky." We never did find out where he came from.

I liked to walk those quiet, shady roads there in the mountains, but almost all of the neighbors had large guard dogs running loose. It would not be a pleasant or peaceful walk under those circumstances. That was, until Rocky came along, and then things were quite different. Whenever I stepped outside, he would be waiting for me. He'd pad right along beside me wherever I walked. If any German shepherds or other large, scary dogs would appear, Rocky would run them off. After a while, the other dogs knew to leave us alone, and they kept still and quiet when we passed. I feared no evil. I had my own personal body guard. Or maybe Rocky was a guardian angel?

16

As a bird out of the snare of the fowlers; the snare is broken, and we are escaped.

—Psalm 124:7

One time, our organization, the Australian Christian Youth Association, placed a large overseas order for the printing of some devotional books. The consignment was shipped from Hong Kong to Sydney. For some unknown reason, the paperwork we needed in order to clear the shipment through customs was delayed in reaching us. Sometimes in missionary work, stranger things happen than even in the world of espionage.

Someone—who perhaps took exception to religious material entering the very *un*spiritual, secular nation of Australia—had gotten ahold of our paperwork and marked the shipment as "objectionable." This term was reserved for items deemed to be seditious, pornographic or otherwise not welcome. Whether this action was intentionally malicious, or just the result of garden-variety bureaucratic incompetence was unclear, and inconsequential. In either case, the cargo was destined to be destroyed within 24 hours. The situation seemed to be quite *hopeless*, someone commented.

Several thousands of dollars had been invested in this purchase which was about to go up in smoke. I was assigned to try to secure the release of our books. At this stage of my life I was young and out to change the world and demonstrate my brilliance. I ran smack into the prevailing Australian attitude that personal ambition was a repugnant social ill, to be avoided and/or at the very least, downplayed at all costs.

Bright and early the next morning—before dawn actually—I showed up at the dock with my rented truck and my pushy Yankee attitude. I found myself at the back of a huge line of trucks (or "queue" as it is known there), some of them quite massive. Given the ambient pace of work, it appeared I would be there all day. In desperation I walked to the front of the line and found a customs agent, and pleaded with him that it was really important that I get my lot cleared today. He eloquently shrugged and pointed to the line of trucks ahead of me and walked off.

While I was steaming and brooding in the stagnant line of trucks, I had an epiphany: *when in Rome, do as the Romans.* In this instance, it was also a case of the Greeks having conquered the Romans. I sauntered back up to the customs office and found a different agent upon whom I would pitch my revised appeal for preferential treatment. In as uncaring, nonchalant and uninterested a mien as I could fabricate, I conspiratorially confided that I was paid for the whole day to clear my shipment through customs and if I got done early I could spend the rest of the day at the beach, at the company's expense. "Good on ya, mate!" was the hearty response, as the sympathetic official promptly directed me to bypass the long line of waiting trucks and come up front for priority clearing. I had cleared the first big hurdle.

Now the greater challenge was to convince the customs authorities that my shipment was not in any way objectionable, and thus should be rescued from destruction. I had a copy of the book we were importing with me, and had bookmarked some of the pages for referral.

I was assigned to meet with a miniscule, elderly gentleman in the second cubicle. My mom had been a great fan of all the Catholic saints.   One of her very favorites was St. Jude, "The Patron Saint of Hopeless Cases." While I was seated in the little civil servant's office, filling out more paperwork, I noticed a holy card pinned to the man's bulletin board. The official must have been one of those rare fervent Catholics in Australia. The card was a likeness of Saint Jude, that "patron saint of hopeless causes!" I was reminded of that comment someone had made the day before, about our situation being "hopeless."

I pleaded my case with this gentleman, and had him read the passages I had marked. Meanwhile, I silently prayed. Somewhat moved by what he read, even if not fully comprehending it, the little customs man exclaimed, "These are like Bibles!" I wholeheartedly agreed with him, nodding and smiling.

He reached into the farthest recesses of his old desk, searching for a particular rubber stamp. When he had found it and inked it up properly, he stamped my application with a resounding "thud" of approval. I rushed out of his office, after thanking him profusely and headed to the next station, where I was able to secure the release of our shipment, just in time.

17.

Surely the wrath of man shall praise thee . . .

—Psalm 76:10

In order to hear the beautiful music, your radio must be tuned to the correct station. Similarly, in order to receive protection and blessings from the Creator, one must be tuned into the proper spiritual wavelength. One day I wasn't.

Someone had seriously wronged my family. Great hurt had been caused. I felt nothing but anger and hatred towards this person for doing so. A black cloud of these dark emotions hung over me. We lived on a remote island along the coast of Southern China, near Hong Kong, at the time and had a small property that we worked hard to keep from being overrun by the lush subtropical vegetation which grew rampant in the summer months. We had no power tools. We used hand tools. For chopping down the thick reed-like grasses that grew four feet tall, we used a big, sturdy hoe with a long wooden handle and a very heavy, sharp iron blade. It was great exercise.

Out I went one afternoon to chop back some of the thick foliage that was forging its way up the steep hillside below our front patio. I was young then, and not as cautious as I am now. ("Oh, you mean, 'young and stupid'?" You would be correct in your assessment.) I did not have sturdy boots on my feet, even though snakes were quite prevalent. It was very hot and very humid. Any extra clothing was uncomfortable to wear, thus I had just rubber flip-flops for footwear.

I was chopping away, clearing the weeds and getting a good workout, a win-win situation. Until that dark cloud once again settled over me and thoughts of anger, bitterness and revenge overtook me. As my emotions were stirred, I chopped harder and harder at the thick, stubborn plants. In the depths of my funk, I took one mighty swing at one particularly thick clump of tall sawgrass, and missed. My footing had slipped on the steep, wet hillside. Instead of uprooting the pesky plant, the downward arc of my swing found the base of my left leg, where it joined to my foot. For the precise location, if you find a medical chart, that spot is called the inferior extensor retinaculum.

I knew I had taken a mighty swing. I knew the edge of the blade of the hoe was very sharp. I knew the metal was very heavy and thick. I knew I was not wearing any protection on my foot. And I knew that I was in the wrong spirit, the wrong frame of mind. I knew that I had disobeyed the warning from Ephesians 4:30 to "grieve not the Holy Spirit of God."

I firmly believed in the power of Supernatural healing and had often been the blessed recipient of such grace. However, I knew this was not a time when I could come boldly before the Throne of Grace. Finally, I also could not bring myself to look at the damage I had done to my foot. I was certain it was horrific, and being of squeamish nature when it comes to all things medical, I was convinced I would simply faint at the sight, and then I would not be able to get back up the hill to safety.

So I closed my eyes and prayed as fervently as I ever had, acknowledging my sins of anger and hatred. I asked for God to renew a proper spirit within me. In a quite obvious demonstration, I was only harming myself by remaining in this state of mind. The pain in my foot was nearly unbearable. Perhaps you have experienced the shock of narrowly avoiding a car accident because your mind was not properly focused? Perhaps you were worried or upset about some person or situation, and thus your mind was not able to operate at normal, optimum levels?

I prayed a prayer of repentance, as King David had once done so many centuries ago, as is recorded in the fifty-first psalm:

> *Have mercy upon me, O God, according to thy lovingkindness: according unto the multitude of thy tender mercies, blot out my*

transgressions. Wash me thoroughly from mine iniquity, and cleanse me from my sin.

For I acknowledge my transgressions: and my sin is ever before me. Against thee, and thee only, have I sinned, and done this evil in thy sight: that thou mightest be justified when thou speakest, and be clear when thou judgest . . .

Behold, thou desirest truth in the inward parts: and in the hidden part thou shalt make me to know wisdom.

Purge me, and I shall be clean: wash me, and I shall be whiter than snow. Make me to hear joy and gladness; that the bones which thou hast broken may rejoice. Hide thy face from my sins, and blot out all mine iniquities.

*Create in me a clean heart, O God; and **renew a right spirit within me.** Cast me not away from thy presence; and take not thy holy spirit from me.*

Restore unto me the joy of thy salvation; and uphold me with thy free spirit. Then will I teach transgressors thy ways; and sinners shall be converted unto thee.

Deliver me from blood guiltiness, O God, thou God of my salvation: and my tongue shall sing aloud of thy righteousness. O Lord, open thou my lips; and my mouth shall shew forth thy praise.

For thou desirest not sacrifice; else would I give it: thou delightest not in burnt offering. The sacrifices of God are a broken spirit: a broken and a contrite heart, O God, thou wilt not despise.

After I finished pouring out my soul, I then tended to the immediate matter at hand—my foot. It took considerable effort and strength to pull the blade of the hoe from within my left foot where it had been imbedded. As the metal blade exited the wound, no blood spurted out. This was a relief, as I was bracing myself for a faint-inducing gush. There was no blood at all. There was also no longer the intense pain.

On further examination, I found that there was no mark at all on my left foot. It was as if it had never happened!

18

Because thou hast made the Lord, who is my refuge, even the Most High, thy habitation, There shall no evil befall thee, neither shall any plague come nigh thy dwelling. For he shall give his angels charge over thee, to keep thee in all thy ways.

—Psalm 91:9-11

This next story may read more like a chapter out of a spy novel. The Old Testament has many references to spies. Joshua chapter 6 is just one such well-known tale. If you have ever experienced living in countries that are hostile to the Gospel, then none of this will seem terribly far-fetched. However, if your personal definition of religious persecution happens to be that you are offended when Methodists make jokes about your fellow Baptists, then you may be in for quite the enlightenment.

For eleven years, I manned a logistics station in Hong Kong for missionaries in the South China region. Our office served folks who ministered in countries closed or hostile to Christian evangelism by facilitating the flow of mail, gifts, finances and personnel when and where normal, official channels were unavailable, or a hindrance.

At one point in the early 1980s, we helped sponsor and organize a radio program that beamed Gospel music and teachings behind the Bamboo Curtain into the southern provinces of China. The response from the listeners was fantastic and enthusiastic. Soon, many who had lived their entire lives in the spiritual vacuum of Communist China were hearing, and receiving the Christian Gospel for the first time. Folks were getting saved—receiving Jesus as their personal Lord and Savior—by the hundreds.

These folks began telling their family, friends and neighbors, and some of them hosted meetings where lay preachers and Christian musicians from the West visited them. Now the salvations were occurring by the thousands. A mail correspondence Gospel education and missionary training program was set up. Staff in nearby Macau kept busy answering scores of letters each day. As word of this success grew, so did the donations pouring in from around the world, from people who could not travel as missionaries themselves, but who wanted to support those who could.

In China, each neighborhood has its local official representing the central Communist Party. These officials are tasked with implementing and enforcing state policies and recruiting support for the Party. In areas that were experiencing an outbreak of the Gospel, folks were suddenly less interested in turning up for propaganda meetings and party recruitment. This augured ill for the local officials who had goals and quotas to meet, in order to ensure their livelihood and indeed their personal safety. Red flags of concern started popping up all around Guangdong province.

In the grand scheme of things, these events might have passed as flea bites on a sleeping dog. But the dog started scratching furiously. This happened to be a very delicate time, when British and Chinese negotiators were locked in protracted and thorny discussions over the future of Hong Kong. Britain wanted to retain possession of their very lucrative colony, but Red China wanted it back. Both sides were very careful not to upset the status quo in any way that might compromise their own bargaining position. Word of the Gospel incursion reached Beijing officials, who put pressure on Hong Kong authorities to do something about this. The Chinese wanted order restored, that is, their order of things.

Sadly, the British, who had once boldly championed the spread of the Gospel around the world, were now only too happy to comply with this demand to silence the missionaries in Hong Kong, in a vain hope that doing so would appease the Chinese, and thus help in their negotiations to keep Hong Kong. In hindsight, we now know how that worked out for them: Great Britain lost all of Hong Kong in 1997. All compromises made regarding civil liberties only served to strengthen Chinese resolve.

So now our missionary "fleas" were being hunted down by both the Chinese dragon and the British lion. Verse thirteen of the ninety-first Psalm makes a curious promise, very apt for this occasion: *the young lion and the dragon shalt thou trample under feet.* I would claim this promise of protection more than once over the coming days.

My responsibility at the logistics office in Hong Kong was to ensure the absolute safety of personnel files, donor lists, and contact information. As such, I kept my office location strictly unknown to virtually everyone. I kept a backup of all files in safe deposit boxes far away, in case I needed to destroy copies I had on hand. Matches and a burn barrel were never far away. These were the days long before flash drives and cloud servers. Microfilm was the highest level of technical security available at that time.

Our missionaries living in Hong Kong were used to entertaining visitors who were interested or curious about our Western beliefs. There was still a certain degree of freedom within the British territory. So it was not unusual when one young man, going by the name of Rudolph, showed up one day, enthusiastic to learn all that our lay preachers could teach him.

His fondness of the Gospel seemed to be matched with an equal interest in meeting as many of our fellow missionaries as possible, so Rudolph was assisted in visiting the various schools and churches scattered around Hong Kong Island, the Kowloon peninsula, and the villages of the New Territories. These visits went on for weeks, if not months.

One morning, while compiling monthly statistical reports and listening to RTHK radio news, I was very startled to hear my own name mentioned! The report spoke in uncomplimentary terms about a "shadowy figure" who was behind the operations of the offensive Gospel incursion into China and elsewhere. If anyone knew of his whereabouts, they were urged to contact authorities immediately. This report happened at about the same time that young convert Rudolph offhandedly asked some folks if there was someone in charge, coordinating all the local missionary activities.

Two emotions surfaced. I was of course, quite anxious for my personal safety, and that of my own immediate family. Sudden deportation was the least serious consequence I was facing. At the same time, I was buoyed by a surrealistic sense of relief. At considerable effort and personal inconvenience and sacrifice, I had diligently and consistently kept my personal whereabouts, and identity, unknown. My employment and visa cover was iron-clad. The address on all my employment and taxation records was a dummy address of an apartment I rented solely for that purpose. Those I served behind the scenes would be able in all honesty to answer that they knew nothing of me, or my location and its goldmine of names, addresses, banking connections, phone numbers and so forth.

As it turns out, Rudolph was a young undercover detective, working for the Royal Hong Kong Police. Once he had completed his mission of visiting every single missionary center in the territory (that is, with the salient exception of mine) a midnight raid was conducted simultaneously at each location. A squad of officers descended on each home. An officer was set at each location to prevent anyone from using the telephone to call for help, or alert others to the danger. (This was long before the days of cell phones.) Police were stationed at all the entrances to prevent any entering or leaving of the locations.

They were after just one piece of information: my location. Everyone was interrogated with that goal in mind. Recordings on answering machines were listened to. In one very depraved and sinister incident, a young Chinese woman, very much pregnant and due to give birth was "questioned" by a team of detectives. One of the men held her down on the ground, while the other menacingly waved an axe back and forth over her swollen abdomen, alluding to the safety of her unborn child. She persisted in telling the truth: she knew nothing about this person they fervently sought. Thankfully, she was released unharmed, albeit traumatized.

They never did find out who I was or where I lived. All of the sensitive information I possessed remained intact. Some missionaries chose to move to other countries and resume activities in friendlier climes. The local Chinese Christians stayed, and remained faithful to their beliefs. Contrary to Mao's belief that he could "eliminate religion" in China, today there are approximately 100 million Christians in China. And the number grows every day.

Now when the high priest and the captain of the temple and the chief priests heard these things, they doubted of them whereunto this would grow. Then came one and told them, saying, Behold, the men whom ye put in prison are standing in the temple, and teaching the people.

Then went the captain with the officers, and brought them before the council: and the high priest asked them, Saying, Did not we straightly command you that ye should not teach in this name? And, behold, ye have filled Jerusalem with your doctrine, and intend to bring this man's blood upon us.

*Then Peter and the other apostles answered and said, **"we ought to obey God rather than men."***

When they had called the apostles, and beaten them, they commanded that they should not speak in the name of Jesus, and let them go.   And they departed from the presence of the council, rejoicing that they were counted worthy to suffer shame for his name. And daily in the temple, and in every house, they ceased not to teach and preach Jesus Christ.

—Acts, chapter 5,
excerpts from verses 24 - 42.

19.

The people that walked in darkness have seen a great light; they that dwell in the land of the shadow of death, upon them hath the light shined.

—Isaiah 9:2

The Iron Curtain, symbolized by the Berlin Wall, fell on November 9th, 1989. Prior to that time, all of the missionaries I knew who operated within those lands to the east of that geopolitical barrier did so clandestinely, out of fear for their lives and for those to whom they cautiously ministered. Everything changed as the new decade of the '90s began.

I relocated to Vienna, Austria, to oversee field operations under these altered circumstances. The first lesson the experienced missionaries had to learn was to cease crawling on their knees and glancing over their shoulder. There were no longer networks of secret police, watching their every move. In their stead were the millions of confused and spiritually empty. Only those citizens older than 72 years of age had any prior, first-hand knowledge of the Gospel, from the days before the Communists had first supplanted the former Christian faith.

In 1991 the Greeks conquered the Russians. More specifically, Boris Yeltsin, the new Russian President, sold *Pravda*, the newspaper that had been the official voice of the Communist Party of the Soviet Union, to a Greek business family. The newspaper was no longer churning out its former prodigious output of Communist propaganda. They were looking for new business.

Prior to this time, the missionaries smuggled one or two copies of a Gospel tract on their person to avoid detection at the tight customs barriers. Now, they could bring in truckloads of Bibles if they wished. The transformation of the landscape was dizzying.

Someone who had heard of the demise of *Pravda* suggested contacting them to print the Gospel of John in massive quantities, something they could do quite easily with their giant printing presses. Labor was cheap in Russia and the ruble was not a strong currency. Production costs were much lower than in Western Europe. Before long, a contract had been signed to print one million copies of the Gospel. And that is the Gospel truth!

One image has remained with me throughout the decades. It was a story related to me by one of the many lay preachers who had set up shop in Russia where they offered seminars to those who wished to learn how to better share their new-found faith in Christ with their friends back in their villages. Into one such seminar, an elderly woman walked haltingly and seemingly in pain. She had traveled a great distance by train to get there.

She meekly approached the people leading the seminar, saying nothing. She opened her heavy winter coat, and began to pull at the stitching of the lining with her thin, aged finger, laboriously unravelling it. Once she had the lining separated from her coat, she reached inside and began pulling out crumpled pieces of old paper money that had been stuffed inside.

Spreading the money on the table, she simply asked, "How many Gospels will this buy?" Her village had collected all the spare money they had and sent this woman on a mission to bring back the long-forbidden Word of God.

A decade later, when I told this experience to my local Congressman, he was bewildered. "Why were people so desperate to hear about Jesus?" I was taken aback by his apparent absence of spiritual depth. He wanted an answer that could be found in any standard psychology textbook. I mention this as a partial answer to the question folks often ask, "What is wrong with America today?"

> *He hath filled the hungry with good things;*
> *and the rich he hath sent empty away.*
> —*Luke 1:53*

20.

In thee, O LORD, do I put my trust. Bow down thine ear to me; deliver me speedily. Into thy hand I commit my spirit. I will be glad and rejoice in thy mercy: for thou hast considered my trouble. For my life is spent. My times are in thy hand.

—*Psalm 31. –excerpts*

My mother passed away on the first day of spring. She loved the springtime best of all the seasons, so it seemed fitting that her last day in this world was March 22nd. While I and my family dearly miss her, my mom's departure was not a sad event, at least not for a believing Christian.

My mom had pretty much been counting the days until she would be called home to Heaven from the time my dad passed away seventeen months prior. I called her every morning at 10 a.m., and we would chat for a few minutes. She was in a retirement community in Florida; I was in Texas. Some days she would say "Beam me up, Lord!" and other times she would say, "I just want to be in Heaven with Daddy."

My mother was in pretty good health, so there was really no immediate end in sight for her stay on this earth. But she was bored, lonely, and missed being able to have her own house. Her children were all grown, and she had no immediate responsibilities.

Often when we talked, she asked me to pray for the Lord to take her Home. I would usually try to steer her onto other subject matters. She was relatively free of any bitterness and usually tried to be cheerful. She appeared to have no fear of death, or dying. Her request presented me with a vexing challenge. Short of her having a sudden, tragic accident, a quick departure from this life seemed unfeasible. And she did not maintain that active of a lifestyle where such risks were likely to occur.

For a while, I ignored her requests, but when she persisted, I felt I should get serious in prayer with the Lord about the matter. So I talked things out with my Creator, something like this:

Lord, my mom loves you, but has grown weary of this life. There really isn't much in this world that interests her any longer. I really don't know how to go about framing her request into a prayer. She would like to go sooner, rather than later. (She is the impatient sort.) I love her, and love being able to talk with her each day; but honestly, there is not much that either one of us can do for the other, or wants done. She has lived a full life, and is content that all her children and grandchildren are doing well. She feels her job is done here.

I leave the matter in your hands. My mom is not the type who would jump off a roof, or slit her wrists, or take a bunch of sleeping pills. She trusts in you. Perhaps there is a way that You can figure this out, the best way possible. You know best.

Shortly thereafter, my mom got sick with a bad cold. She received immediate attention and treatment, but did not improve much. She became quite weak and dehydrated and had to be transferred to the nearby hospital. There, I think my mom saw her way out. She had lost her appetite and pretty much refused to eat or drink anything further. After a few days, her condition deteriorated, and she was transferred to the same hospice where my dad had spent his last days. The hospice staff is wonderful and my mom probably felt quite "at home" there, much more so than being at the hospital. Within a week, she would have her wish.

A few significant events transpired before my mom's departure. My two sisters were both there with her during those final days and we remained in constant contact. On one of the last days, I was headed to the city with my youngest son "P.J." who was scheduled to have oral surgery. I was of two minds: as a parent, I was concerned that all would go well with my son's surgery; as a son, I was on standby for news of any major change in my mother's condition. As I was about to pull out of the driveway, my wife called me to come back into the house. My mom was on the phone and wanted to let us know that she had just seen Suzy standing at the end of her bed, smiling at her.

Suzy was my oldest daughter, who had tragically passed away a couple years prior. My mom really loved Suzy. In her darkest days, Suzy would declare that she no longer believed in God. She said she could not reconcile how a loving God could let people do such bad things to others. This was not an argument I was ever able to win with her. That type of reconciliation and understanding can only come from within, in the heart, and not through reasoning of the mind.

The fact that Suzy appeared to my mom, and smiling at the end of my mom's bed was a double comfort: I knew that my daughter now understood things clearly from the Other Side; and it was my mom's time to go, as Suzy had come for her, to welcome her Home.

Before my mom passed away, she did an astounding thing: she picked her pallbearers and insisted on getting a gift for each of the six of them, and wanted to write them each a thank you letter. My sister Jude was the scribe and actually took my mom's dictation. Many folks remarked on what an exceptional gesture my mom had made. My mom's last act became the inspiration for the book I never planned to write, but which came to me pretty much in a flash that night between her visitation hours and the funeral the next day. I dedicated that book to my mom and dad. Perhaps you have heard of it, *Just Good Clean Fun.*

* * * * *

First Corinthians 15:19 states, *If in* **this** *life only we have hope in Christ, we are of all men most miserable.*

Here I am going to allow my preaching to go to meddling. Daily I see commercials on TV, promising people a few months more life, if they take some new, experimental, and quite likely, expensive drug. "Who **wouldn't** want to live longer?" the ad challenges. I think that depends on your belief, and your values. If you believe that life ends at death, you might wish to prolong the inevitable as long as possible.

At a certain point, the *quality* of life must come into play. The tallest person is not necessarily the healthiest. The heaviest person is not automatically the strongest. The person who spent the most years in college is not necessarily the most intelligent. So, in like fashion, the person who lives the longest is not necessarily the happiest, the most productive, or the most beneficial.

If, as a Christian, or a person of another faith, one believes in a better world to come in the Hereafter, then it would seem reasonable *not* to claw and cling to this earthly existence for as long as possible, at all costs. A young mother who has small children to raise, might want to fight harder to survive, for their sakes. A man in his nineties, who currently has no projects or plans of any import in the works, might have less of a valid reason to seek all sorts of expensive medical and pharmaceutical treatments so as to simply live one more day.

Even if one claimed not to believe in a God, and only believed in caring for other humans in this life, some of these same arguments would still hold true. If one did really love their surviving family members, why put them through months and years of anxiety and drama and spend all of their potential inheritance? Why not let them get on with their own lives, rather than be preoccupied with watching you die? Why burn through all the money that was earned and saved so diligently for decades in a just few weeks of costly terminal care? And to what avail? Could the answer be that some folks, despite their professed claim to atheism, are scared that there *really* is a Hell, and know that they deserve to go there.

This medical trend—trying to extend life at advanced years for as long as possible, and at all costs—is predicated on two current prevailing sentiments: "more is better" and "you deserve better."

The "more is better" mantra is nothing more than a product of consumerism marketing. A burger that is really already too large to be healthful for you can be "supersized." A house that is already bigger than is necessary can be added on to for a grander appearance of affluence. Otherwise perfectly fine body parts are enhanced so their owners can better compete for jobs, mates, or attention. Countering this trend are dozens of other cultures with billions of people who would argue that *quality* is much more important than quantity. Many of them consider such excess to be tasteless, anti-social, or even sinful and/or immoral.

The "you deserve better" mantra is a lie perpetrated on young minds from their start, molding them into whining narcissists who complain at every turn that someone else got a better deal than they did— whether it is a fancier car, a better cell phone or a more expensive prom outfit—none of which was earned, and by the way, none of which was "deserved." Meanwhile, billions in Third World countries would love to have the "miserable" life that these ungrateful souls complain about. It would be a dream to live in such luxury and safety.

The argument may be advanced that it is their personal choice to spend millions to live a few weeks longer; that it isn't hurting anyone else, since it is "their money." Have you considered the current cost of your health insurance premiums? Excessive, elective surgery uses up valuable resources and ties up expensive medical personnel, driving up the cost of essential health care for everyone. I might struggle to cover necessary dental expenses that my company's healthcare plan doesn't cover. Meanwhile, someone incarcerated for a violent crime can have elective and very expensive "gender reassignment" surgery provided free of charge, that is, in other words, at the expense of the law-abiding taxpayers not behind bars, who are working hard to keep a roof over their heads.

Once a society loses sight of acknowledging and heeding the Will of the Creator, it becomes a ship adrift, without a rudder, without a captain, without a compass, map or destination. It's "every man for himself." In other words, *chaos reigns.*

* * * * * * *

Often, the argument advanced from some pulpits is that "God works in partnership with the doctors." This is a very cozy, convenient compromise where no one is offended. Tithes keep coming in, the flow not upset by those who would have had their lack of faith challenged, or by the medical professionals feeling slighted. One point lacking in this argument is any documentation that proves God has signed on to this deal. New Testament teachings suggest otherwise:

A certain woman, which had an issue of blood twelve years and had suffered many things of many physicians, and had spent all that she had, and was nothing bettered, but rather grew worse,

When she had heard of Jesus, came in the press behind, and touched his garment. For she said, if I may touch but his clothes, I shall be whole. And straightway the fountain of her blood was dried up; and she felt in her body that she was healed of that plague.

And Jesus, immediately knowing in himself that virtue had gone out of him, turned him about in the press, and said, who touched my clothes? . . . And he looked round about to see her that had done this thing.

But the woman, fearing and trembling, knowing what was done in her, came and fell down before him, and told him all the truth. And he said unto her, Daughter, thy faith hath made thee whole; go in peace, and be whole of thy plague.

—*Mark 5:25-34*

Notice that the Lord did *not* say, "My garment has healed you" or "my Father works in partnership with the tailor of my garment." Her *faith* alone is what made her whole.

* * * * * * *

Having lost this argument about partnership between the Divine and the doctors, the final white flag goes up from those who defend the faithless, with this old saw: "Well, the day of miracles is past."

Really, now? Have those who spew such poison ever taken the time to consider the miracle of life—of conception and birth—events that happen by the millions each week? No, the true reason for this dearth of healing experiences was explained by the evangelist over two thousand years ago:

And He did not many mighty works there
*because of their **unbelief.***
—Matthew 13:58

21.

Out of the depths have I cried unto thee, O Lord. Lord, hear my voice; let thine ears be attentive to the voice of my supplications.

—Psalm 130:1-2

This story contains three miraculous elements. It took place in the remote Tung Hang Mei Valley of Lantau Island near Hong Kong. Hong Kong is very crowded. It resembles Manhattan, having six million people crowded into tall buildings on a tiny plot of prime real estate. In stark contrast, the tiny valley where we lived, just twelve miles away, had a grand total of six houses.

My young family had lived in those tall skinny residential towers. Most folks did. 99% of the folks in Hong Kong lived in tiny apartments. Only the few privileged wealthy and powerful had private homes. The only patch of grass we were familiar with was the small square of lawn in the Royal Botanical Gardens which guarded on all four sides with warning placards, *Keep Off the Grass!*

As our family grew in size and number, we moved to an apartment on the less crowded, peaceful Lantau Island. It was still an apartment, but now we were on the second floor, instead of the 21st floor. The "traffic" outside our window now only consisted of pushcarts and water buffaloes, a welcome relief from the endless flow of taxis, double-decker buses and smoky diesel trucks which over the years we had come to accept as inevitable "background noise." But there was still no grass: just a small concrete patio surrounded by a concrete wall. But this was close enough to heaven by comparison for our purposes.

One day, while walking the trails of Lantau Island, we were approached by a young relative of our landlord. "Would you like to rent a house that has a swimming pool?" he enquired. He might as well have asked us, "Would you like to have wings to fly?" Not only were there very few houses in Hong Kong, there were even fewer swimming pools. Certainly nothing we could afford as missionaries, such as membership to the Royal Hong Kong Yacht Club.

It was very hot and very humid in Hong Kong most of the year. The only places to cool off were at the crowded and rather dirty beaches. Naturally, we were very intrigued by the possibility he offered, regardless of how far-fetched it might seem. So we followed him for about thirty minutes as he led us along the winding, narrow concrete pathways of the island and up into the hillside.

And there it was, at the end of the path just beyond a red gate! A middle-aged Chinese gentleman had lived there for over twenty years. He had carved a beautiful home out of the wild, raw hillside of the isolated Tung Hang Mei Valley. Up a long, narrow trail that clung to the steep hillside, he had cut back the bamboo overgrowth and hauled cement, sand and water to painstakingly build a solid, half-mile-long concrete pathway to his home. He built a gate at the entrance to his property, as was traditional. There was no fence around the property, as was also traditional. Native bamboo grew dense and tall, providing natural privacy and protection for the one-acre clearing of the steep hillside.

This man went on to build a two-story reinforced concrete home, and added a patio around the south and west sides of the building. He found a natural spring two hundred meters further up the mountainside and built a small stone dam to create a private water supply. He placed steel piping down the slope to a 250-gallon tank he had built of stone and concrete. Later on, he extended the pipelines so as to water the crops and trees he planted. He added a large stone fish tank, dug into the hillside, which doubled as an emergency reserve of water during the autumn dry spells. This structure was about six feet deep, 45 feet long and twenty feet across. For all intents and purposes, it was a swimming pool.

He planted twelve varieties of trees, planning it such that a different tree produced its fruit on each of the twelve months, thus he always had fresh fruit to pick while he was working. (Shades of Revelations 22:2?, *In the midst of the street of it, and on either side of the river, was there the tree of life, which bare* **twelve manner of fruits**, *and yielded her fruit every month.*)

In the valley was a cluster of banana plants, kept well-watered and fertilized from the bathroom runoff. Another trough carried waste water from the kitchen down to the neatly terraced vegetable beds. A huge, flowering Flame of the Forest tree shaded most of the front patio and the house, providing welcome coolness in the summer. This was as close to Heaven as you could get in Hong Kong.

Across the picturesque valley, the waterfalls roared during the rainy season. The valley was completely surrounded by steep, granite mountains, covered halfway up their slopes with thick shrubs, small trees and undergrowth. Only a very narrow break in the circular ring of mountains allowed for passage *in* to the secluded valley, and passage *out* of the valley for the stream that flowed down to Silvermine Bay, and eventually the South China Sea. Towering in the distance was the majestic Lantau Peak, often shrouded with misty clouds. This unknown man's home was a miniature, private paradise.

Yet amazingly enough, after years of labor to complete this herculean task by himself, the owner now had inexplicable yearnings to return to the rural countryside of his ancestral homeland in

Mainland Communist China. One bright spring morning, he set off, after first putting his affairs in order and letting the local police sergeant know. He was never heard from again in that valley. His home had been vacant for a year. It was available for rent, for $385 per month. This was much less than we paid in rent for a tiny 200-square-foot apartment in the crowded city of Hong Kong. We couldn't say "yes!" fast enough. So this was the first miracle: finding a private home with a pool in Hong Kong for a mere pittance.

The second miracle speaks to our inexperience and ignorance, and the merciful Creator's faithfulness. We had little knowledge of the workings of the water system of Hong Kong. We only knew that we turned on the tap and out came the water. We also knew that you had to filter that water first before drinking it, if you did not want to become ill. Beyond that, I knew little of the infrastructure. I had seen pipes lining the pathway further down the valley, and when we turned on the tap at our prospective new home, the water came out. In my mind, I connected the two observations: city water ran to our remote property, albeit with reduced pressure.

After we had moved in, further investigation would show that my conclusion was wrong. The city water pipes stopped well before our property. We were on our own! Being the city slickers that we were, it never dawned on us to ask where the water came from for this remote house on the mountainside. We had simply turned on the tap: when water came out, that was the end of our inspection.

As it turned out, there was no city-supplied water to the property. And there was no well. A few days after we had settled in, I set out to investigate the mysterious source of our delicious-tasting water. A one-inch-thick galvanized steel pipe emerged from the back of the semi-detached kitchen building and I followed that pipe up the hill, past some steps, through tall grass and around trees and shrubs until I came to a concrete water tank.

The civil engineering of this house is quite amazing when you think of all the cement that had to be hauled up the one mile pathway (which itself first had to be constructed) without the aid of cement trucks, or any trucks for that matter. It was carried or pushed by human power: hundreds of thousands of pounds of concrete and sand and rebar for the house alone. Then there were paths, and patios, and another building, and steps, and finally this water tank.

On that hillside was quite an ingenious, private, naturally organic filtration system. There were actually two adjoining concrete tanks, each a cube that was about twenty-four inches per side. Their common wall was pierced with a few holes. In the first tank were large stones; in the second tank, sand. Water came into the higher, primary tank at the top, settled through the stones and emerged into the secondary tank, where the water filtered through the awaiting sand and finally emerged from a pipe at the bottom of the second tank and then headed to the house.

The tank was fifty feet above the level of the house, so the water pressure was adequate. There was a float valve on the intake primary tank to stop the flow of incoming water when the tanks were full. So the next mystery was to find out where the pipe came from *before* it arrived at the tank. This next investigation would first necessitate some serious path cutting.

There were small shrubs dotted along the hillside, but worse were the tall, thick, razor-sharp-edged, unyielding grasses that grew head-high. Machetes worked, as long as you had heavy gloves for protection from cuts. But it was hard work, slow going, and punctuated by the discovery of various snake species. In the heat and humidity, it was only possible to clear a few feet of the pathway alongside the pipeline each day.

Finally, we reached the source of our water! The galvanized pipe was coupled crudely into a short length of larger PVC pipe which was covered with a green vinyl screen. The apparatus sat in a shady shallow rock pool where water collected after emerging from an underground spring a few meters further up the hillside. The flow was gentle, but always constant. After the major hill fire—which I wrote about earlier in this book—all of the plant growth had been reduced to mere ash, leaving just barren soil and rock. Yet this spring faithfully continued to produce cool delicious water without interruption, regardless of the changing seasons.

At the other—delivery—end of the pipeline close to our house was another mystery: a large hole in the ground—forty-five feet long, six feet deep and twenty feet wide. It was made of stone walls of granite rock about one foot cube in size. Where had the rocks come from, and how had someone placed them there without the aid of heavy machinery? Those were but two of my unanswered questions.

The more vexing question was the purpose of the structure. It obviously was to collect water since a spur of the pipeline dumped water into it, and there was a big wooden plug fashioned out of a log at the bottom for a drain. Was it a water reservoir for all the plants and trees on the property? Or had this been a fish pond at one time? In any event, we decided to deem it a swimming pool, and set about to try filling it.

This was the dry season, and no rain would fall for some months. We located a tap near the "pool" and turned it on. The water from that distant spring gurgled its way down the old pipes and trickled into the giant stone structure. It would take tens of thousands of gallons of water to fill it! We left the tap on and went to sleep. The next morning, when we checked, there was nearly half a foot of water in the bottom—fresh, clean and cool. After two weeks, the pool was overflowing. No matter how hot the weather, or how dry the conditions, the stream never ceased its faithful provision of water. This was our second miracle.

These two scenarios speak to miraculous supply and establish the setting for this third miracle, which vividly demonstrates Divine Protection.

Our children became proficient swimmers and enjoyed the pool most every day. In the second year, we added a pool filtration system. There was a four-inch PVC pipe which went to the bottom of the pool as intake for the pump. One day, ten-year-old James decided to investigate the arrangement and dove underneath the surface. I was in the pool with two or three other people at the time. We paid no attention to James, as the kids were accustomed to swimming about on their own quite capably.

We suddenly heard a commotion and a desperate "Help!" James' head briefly appeared above the water and then disappeared. We rushed to his aid. What had happened next astounded us. James had been poking around the PVC pipe and got his arm stuck in the pipe, five feet below the surface. The pump's powerful suction held his arm fast and he could not withdraw it. Under such circumstances, he would silently drown, unnoticed by the adults at the other end of the pool.

Somehow, in a moment of supernatural strength, little James had managed to force his way to the surface, tearing the stout pipe away from the side of the pool. He was not tall enough to stand and have his head above water when he yelled for help. He was swimming, with this pipe firmly attached to his arm, which he bent in the process. One person raced to turn off the pump. Another dove down and extracted James from the pipe's grip while the rest of us began praying. After a few coughs and sputters, the normal color began to reappear on James' pale face. He happily swam off. We immediately installed a child-proof cap on the end of the intake pipe.

The event left us stunned in awed respect. If you have ever (safely) experienced a close lightning strike, then you can approximate an understanding of how we felt. You see the blinding flash, hear the incredible roar of the ensuing thunder and are repulsed by the obnoxious weird smell of the ozone, yet you live to enjoy yet another day of life. Our failure to safely complete the plumbing project and our ignoring of James and Suzy while they frolicked in the pool might have caused a heart-wrenching and life-altering accidental death. But it didn't.

22

But my God shall supply all your need
according to his riches in glory by Christ
Jesus.

—*Philippians 4:19*

Our mission work took us to many countries with vastly differing conditions. What did remain constant throughout our travels was our dependence upon the faithful provision of our loving Creator. Our daily needs were always met somehow. Often, there was nothing dramatic about how it happened. But it always did.

One bright sunny winter day in Sydney, we gathered before breakfast for devotions. At the end there was a time when a list of needs were voiced, and prayed over. That morning the cook asked us to pray for extra bread. We were consuming it more rapidly in the cooler weather, and we had a spiked increase in the number of visitors who stayed for meals.

As we prayed, there was a knock on the front door. I went to see who it was. I can recall vividly walking down the long, narrow hallway with its twelve-foot-high ceiling. This was an old terrace house. The front door was painted a deep green, with tiny panes of glass set into the intricate woodwork. The glass was covered with a frosted pattern. Light could penetrate, but only vague shapes could be seen.

I could perceive that there was a tall person on the front step carrying something large. As I opened the door, a gentleman silently thrust in my direction a large basket filled with the longest loaves of bread I had ever observed. There were dozens of them, each two or three feet long. Before I had the words *thank you* out of my mouth, the donor turned and departed without a word.

> *But when ye pray, use not vain repetitions, as the heathen do: for they think that they shall be heard for their much speaking. Be not ye therefore like unto them: for your Father knoweth what things ye have need of, before ye ask him. After this manner therefore pray ye: Our Father which art in heaven, Hallowed be thy name. Thy kingdom come, Thy will be done in earth, as it is in heaven.*
>
> *Give us this day our daily bread.*
>
> *—Matthew 6: 7-11*

As the Scripture above teaches, our Heavenly Father obviously knew what we needed before we asked that morning. He sent the delivery man ahead of time, to arrive before we could say, "Amen."

About a year later I was living in a "working" class suburb two miles west of downtown Sydney called "Ultimo." As the name might otherwise suggest, there was nothing exceptionally pretty or pleasant about the neighborhood. It was mostly warehouses and busy roads, filled with noisy trucks.

Some folks are history buffs. Others are just plain curious. Either way, the question might arise, *why was this place named Ultimo?* There wasn't much *ultimate* about it. 'Ultimo' was originally the name of the estate of a Dr. John Harris, on 34 acres granted to him by the governor of New South Wales in 1803. The property was named in recognition of a legal clerical error that saved Harris from being court-martialed. His offense was listed as 'ultimo' (meaning, "having occurred in the previous month") when it should have been cited as 'instant' (meaning, "having occurred in the same month").

Well, in this particular instance of time, our little mission home had plenty of bread, and plenty of fruit and vegetables, which we obtained from the Central Market vendors. Our diet lacked sufficient meat. So, as was our wont, we prayed for various needs in our morning devotions. We, of course, did include our request for some good quality meat.

Prayers needed to be said loudly, as the busy street sent wave after wave of industrial noises through the thin, non-insulated window panes of the old stone house. At times it appeared we were shouting at each other in order to be understood. Even louder was a large *bump* heard outside, the sound made when a heavy object falls to the hard pavement. A couple of our folks rushed to the front door, thinking that there may have been an accident, with resulting injury to someone.

When they opened the door, they found no injured person, just a large crate. It had apparently fallen off the back of a truck as it bounced down the rutted, uneven road. The truck was long gone. In its wake, sitting right at our front door, was a large crate. It was filled with dozens of cans of very nice quality meat. It took two men to carry the load into the house, which they presented to our delighted cook.

He said unto Simon, Launch out into the deep,
and let down your nets for a draught. And
Simon answering said unto him, Master, we
have toiled all the night, and have taken
nothing: nevertheless at thy word I will let down
the net. And when they had this done, they
enclosed a great multitude of fishes: and their
net brake. And they beckoned unto their
partners, which were in the other ship, that they
should come and help them. And they came, and
filled both the ships, so that they began to sink.
He was astonished, and all that were with him,
at the draught of the fishes which they had taken.
—Luke 5: 4-9

Simon obeyed the Stranger's seemingly senseless command to let down his nets in waters where there were no fish to be found. Today, some two thousand years later, some folks would say it is mere folly to "talk into thin air" and expect an unseen force to heal, or provide, or direct your path.

Those who dare to put the Scriptures to the test know otherwise. The promises contained therein are not just pretty words designed to render the reader into pious state of being. These promises are alive, and they work—for those who dare to appropriate them.

23.

He that dwelleth in the secret place
of the most High shall abide under
the shadow of the Almighty.
Surely he shall deliver thee from the snare of
the fowler, and from the noisome pestilence.
He shall cover thee with his feathers, and
under his wings shalt thou trust.
Thou shalt not be afraid for the terror by
night; nor for the pestilence
that walketh in darkness;
A thousand shall fall at thy side, and ten
thousand at thy right hand;
but it shall not come nigh thee.

—Psalm 91:1-7, –excerpts.

O ver thirty years, in varying conditions on several continents, we often faced disease and other dangers. Sometimes we were even protected and healed of a disease or poison before we even knew of the danger we faced!

I can remember lying in bed in a backroom of our terrace house in Potts Point, an inner suburb of Sydney, Australia. I had a very intense headache which persisted for several days. I was not prone to migraines; in fact, I rarely got a headache of any type. But on this occasion, if I moved my head in the slightest bit, the pounding was overwhelming. I was also running a high fever.

I drank as much water as I could. I took aspirin on a regular basis. I found it hard to sleep, but reading was unbearable, as my eyes were suddenly very sensitive to light. I tried to remain as still as possible, as whenever I moved it exacerbated the pain in my head. My neck felt like it was gradually turning into stiff metal. Trips to the bathroom were major ordeals and required assistance. I was only in my twenties, but I felt quite ancient and helpless.

Word came to me that some other missionaries in the area we knew had been facing similar symptoms. Perhaps it is true that "misery loves company," as I did feel somewhat relieved that I was not in this strange battle alone. I was not imagining things, nor exaggerating my circumstances. But I was still sick.

After four days, all symptoms and pain passed away. I was restored whole and was able to carry on normal life, as if nothing had ever happened. The others that I spoke to had similar reports to share. We were all puzzled, yet relieved to be healed.

A few days later, we began to read and hear about a major meningitis outbreak which was causing much concern for the local health officials. As you may be aware, those three symptoms I had—fever, headache, sensitivity to light, and neck stiffness—are hallmarks of this sickness. Meningitis is described as potentially life-threatening, with a high mortality rate if left untreated. None of us knew at the time we were battling meningitis; we just all had "bad headaches."

Had we known the seriousness of the disease we were battling, we would certainly have been very concerned for our lives, and sought medical help. In our particular case, perhaps "ignorance was bliss."

* * * * * * *

Another pestilence that a small group of us unknowingly faced while living on the remote Lantau Island near Hong Kong was of the man-made nature. Some of you may be old enough, or else good enough students of history, to recall "Agent Orange," the defoliant used for a decade in the Vietnam War. Once the practice was stopped, another problem emerged: what to do with the tons of leftover, dangerous poison, now a known carcinogen.

Shamefully, what unscrupulous entrepreneurs often do with such banned chemicals and drugs is to offload them on unsuspecting Third World countries for a tidy profit. So, rebranded under a more obscure and innocuous name, this dioxin found its way to the little shops in the rural villages of Southern China where it was touted as a miracle weed killer. The warm, rainy clime of the area caused rapid growth. Weeds and other unwanted plants were very prolific, and quickly choked out gardens and streams.

Earlier on, I described the little hillside spring that fed water to our property. I mentioned the difficulty we had clearing the thick brush in order to maintain a pathway to the water source for maintenance. When the miracle weed killer showed up in our village, we eagerly obtained some and began to spray the thick, jungle-like pathway with the herbicide. All of the lettering on the container was in arcane Chinese characters. This made it doubly certain that we had no idea what we were using.

Within a few days, we rejoiced at the effectiveness of this new product. Gone were the strenuous, painful hours of hacking with machetes and hoes to clear the long pathway! Big, tall, thick grasses and weeds and small shrubs succumbed and dried up and withered away quickly, as if by magic. (One can only image the horrors faced by the farmers of Southeast Asia in the previous decade.)

Our celebration was short-lived. The dioxin made its way into our water source. In the hot weather, we all drank lots of this cold, delicious spring water. This also meant we were consuming large quantities of dioxin! One by one, folks living at our place began to break out with large, and excruciatingly painful boils.

I was one of those. The boils that developed over bony areas were more easily dealt with. I had some which nestled in the soft areas under my arm. The pain was off the chart. It was very hot, very humid and we only had fans for cooling. It was unpleasant to say the least.

I can still vividly recall lying still on my bed on the second floor, hoping for the hillside breeze blowing through the windows to pick up and lessen my misery. At one point, feeling I could not last much longer under such circumstances, I called out to God with my whole heart. "Lord, have mercy on me, and deliver me!"

Suddenly, I was seized with an incredible shaking which frightened me and caused me to quickly forget that I had just prayed for Divine assistance. I felt I was coming to the end. I felt a squeezing and twisting, as if I were a wet rag being wrung out to dry. I needed to vomit and evacuate my bowels urgently, violently, and simultaneously.

Once this was accomplished, and I was showered, I felt a strange sensation: there was absolutely no pain! My constant, unwelcomed companion for the past week departed. I felt around my armpits, and all of the swelling had vanished. I was healed.

When this scourge passed, we took the remaining contents of the container to a chemist, who confirmed that it was indeed recycled Agent Orange. He advised that we have nothing further to do with it! "Use the machetes to cut the grass. You'll live longer."

All of us fully recovered. Three decades later, there have been no incidents of cancer or complications caused by our contact with this deadly substance. The only physical reminder I have today is a small dime-sized discolored patch of skin on my lower left leg. It testifies of a time when I was delivered from an unknown danger by Someone much bigger and wiser than I.

And these signs shall follow them that believe: if they drink any deadly thing, it shall not hurt them; they shall lay hands on the sick, and they shall recover.
—Mark 16:17-18.

24.

Delight thyself also in the Lord: and he shall
give thee the desires of thine heart.

—Psalm 37:4

N ot all is thunder and lightning in the life of
faith. I've recounted some dramatic stories
of deliverance, healing, protection and
miraculous provision of our needs while living a life
of faith as missionaries. But not every touch of the
Divine is so sensational.

Some of the little things, the niceties of life—non-
essential, yet very much welcomed—can provide a
powerful and heartening testimony to the kindness,
gentleness, and thoughtful graciousness of the
Creator. And so I will end on this note, with some of
my fulfilled wishes, those special little things.

Thy gentleness hath made me great.
—Psalm 18:35

Proverbs 4:18 states: *But the path of the just is as the*
shining light, that shineth more and more unto the
perfect day. Some may interpret this to mean that
just—or righteous—people get better and better as
time goes on. I think a more accurate, and humble
view might be that the Creator's blessings keeping
faithfully increasing over time.

I have written about the peaceful, yet remote and isolated Tung Hang Mei Valley on beautiful Lantau Island where my family and I lived for years while stationed in Hong Kong.   The steep, mile-long winding narrow concrete footpath was a daily challenge to navigate: by foot for transportation, and with a pushcart when moving goods to and fro.

By night, the challenge was even greater, as the steep hillsides which surrounded the valley blocked out any light from outside civilization. We had only the light of the moon and the stars for illumination.

Summer days were long, and this was not much of a problem most days. During the winter months though, the days were shortened and night fell quite early, often before we made it home from the ferry ride out of the big city of Hong Kong.

Compounding the frightfulness of the dark was the factor of the unknown: the area was filled with many species of venomous snakes and large spiders and nasty huge centipedes and scorpions. Big webs, suspended between trees, hung across the pathway at night, often with a four-inch-long spider in its midst, awaiting its evening prey. If you ran into the sticky strands in the dark, your face was covered by the macabre stuff and you might be treated to a very close-up look at a pulsating spider.

So we always tried to carry a flashlight with us and also check that the batteries were fresh. It was our weapon of choice against the darkness. It was helpful to grab a walking stick, so as to have it run into the spider webs, and all else that awaited, before we did.

If it ever happened that the flashlight was dropped, or the batteries went dead, the pathway was instantly plunged into darkness. When this happened, we had to grope our way along as best we could, tapping with a stick to make sure we stayed on the narrow path and did not fall off the pathway and into the steep valley below, with all its wilderness night life awaiting the intruder.

One day, while pondering that verse, Proverbs 4:18, in meditation, I was emboldened to request that somehow our path could shine more brightly—literally. We had little contact with the outside utility services. There were only a half-dozen old, simple farmhouses scattered in our valley. The phone, gas, electric, and water utility people were very busy elsewhere trying to keep up with the demand from the burgeoning mass of millions of customers in the metropolis of nearby Hong Kong.

Who would want to run high voltage wiring through wet fields and dense forests for a costly set of street lights to be constructed on a steep, treacherous, narrow rural pathway to service only a handful of low-volume customers? It just wasn't good business sense.

But my Creator is in the business of making the unimaginable happen. Within months of my request there were teams of workers—electricians, concrete workers, engineers, plumbers, construction crews—on my little pathway, feeding the 600 volt lines through thick, galvanized steel conduits bolted to the concrete pathway. Sturdy, tall modern steel poles were spaced out strategically along our path. Soon, in the evenings we were treated to the warm glow of amber-colored lighting, casting a welcoming aura along our little bright pathway in the dark.

We never received any official notice this project would be happening. There was no increase in our monthly utility bills. My only question was: *Why didn't I think to ask for this sooner?*

* * * * * *

Encouraged by the amazing answer to my request for better lighting, I pushed on. The tiny five-hundred-year-old village a mile down the path from our house, where we caught the ferries to other parts of the world, was called MuiWo. It was a tiny collection of improvised metal shacks where merchants plied their goods, sold their produce and offered cooked fast food. I thought it'd be nice to have a western restaurant to add to the cuisine options. When folks came to visit us, we had to squeeze them into some space in the living room. Wouldn't a nice hotel solve both needs? Within a year, I would find out.

Lo and behold, rising from the sandy stretches of quiet Silver Mine Bay Beach, where water buffaloes once roamed, an imposing two-story new hotel was constructed, very modern and with a nice restaurant serving both Chinese and Western fare. Thus the Silvermine Beach Resort was built, very much to the bemused fascination of the local fishermen, farmers and other villagers. It rose like an alien craft in the midst of a wilderness. I checked in among the hotels' very first guests. There was even a lovely, clean pool.

Such an undertaking was certainly a leap of faith for the investors. For some time the hotel remained rather under-utilized. But eventually it became very popular with tourists and weekenders from the city. Recently the hotel underwent extensive renovations. Thirty years on, it is doing a brisk business, which I witnessed first-hand when I last visited Hong Kong two years ago.

* * * * * * *

Missionary service often requires that one foregoes certain luxuries. For me, one of those was golfing. I loved golfing when I was young. On the mission field, the busy schedule usually prevented time for such activities and the limited budgets dictated against such non-essential expenses.

Fifteen years into my missionary work, bulldozers began rumbling on the distant mountaintop across the valley from our home in Tung Hang Mei Valley. The peaceful atmosphere of the sleepy agricultural life on Lantau Island was shattered by the roar of heavy earthmoving equipment. Our family went on weekly hikes throughout the mountains on the many trails that crisscrossed those slopes. Our curiosity aroused, we set out to explore one Saturday morning. What we discovered seemed as bizarre as the first lunar landing must have appeared.

"This can't be!" I was amazed. There, on that remote mountaintop that had remained undisturbed for many millennia, an 18-hole golf course was being carved out for the nouveau riche of Hong Kong and China. Being a westerner, a rarity in these parts, I was afforded special treatment as a potential customer, and once the course was completed, I was able to play several complimentary rounds with a colleague.

The vistas were breathtaking, with the busy waters of the South China Sea far below surrounding the lofty plateau. It was a very special treat, being my first time reveling in the creation's beauty while golfing since I had personally encountered the Creator.

Another fifteen years later I would retire from active mission work overseas. My wife and I settled in East Texas and went about establishing a home for our houseful of growing young children. There was much to do fixing up the old farm property, earning a living and homeschooling our future college graduates.

A few years into our stay in our adopted home town, I had one of those moments while commuting from work. *It sure would be nice to have a golf course near home where I could grab some relaxation and get some healthful exercise.* There were expensive country clubs 45 minutes away—too far, too costly.

Then one day, the military downsized its presence at the nearby Red River Army Depot. It had been built at the start of WWII and was in continual operation since then. Now the operation would be handled by civil contractors with just one commanding officer on-site. Gone was the need for the former officers' mess and the officers' private golf course.

The course was sold to a local property developer and was then opened to the public. It was just five minutes' drive from my house and very inexpensive. When I heard the news, I was just as flabbergasted as I was that day fifteen years ago on Lantau Island, watching a new golf course being constructed on that isolated mountain top.

The now-public golf course in our area also had an Olympic-sized pool. Yearly family membership was not expensive and our vanload of kids all enjoyed swimming there for several happy summers. With five kids, the set family fee was a real bargain!

Now, when God moves bulldozers in the South China Sea, that is an amazing feat. But for the U.S. Army to turn over its golf course so that I could play there, well, that is something else!

* * * * * *

One last such Divine kindness I will share with you involves another luxury that I had to forego all those years as a missionary. When I was a student at MIT—where this story began in Chapter One—I very much enjoyed attending the weekly concerts by the Boston Symphony Orchestra. I loved classical music.

When I retired and we settled near Texarkana, I found that there was no symphony orchestra within 200 miles. It was a bit of a cultural desert. It was not a large city and it was only logical that it could not easily support such a major endeavor. However, one day I sighed while working in the yard, *it would be so nice to be able to hear symphonic music played once in a while!*

A few years later, some civic minded individuals put together funding to start the Texarkana Symphony Orchestra (TSO). They already had a perfect venue for the performances—the newly renovated and rebranded Perot Theatre, formerly the flagship of the Saenger theatre chain in the South. It has beautifully ornate décor and wonderful acoustics.

On September 11th, 2001, early that morning before the planes crashed into the World Trade Centre, Mr. Marc-André Bougie, the future conductor of the TSO arrived from Canada. Marc-André is an extremely talented gentleman with a teacher's heart. Maestro Bougie is as warm-hearted and humble an individual as he is talented.

Over the past ten years the Texarkana Symphony Orchestra has matured into a wonderful venue for fine music to be enjoyed. I have been able to enjoy many fine concerts there. I also have the privilege of the personal friendship with this fine man. Once again the scriptural promise is fulfilled:

> *"The things which are impossible with men are possible with God."* —Luke 18:27.

* * * * * * *

Yea, though I walk through the valley of the shadow of death, I will fear no evil: for thou art with me; thy rod and thy staff they comfort me.

Thou preparest a table before me in the presence of mine enemies: thou anointest my head with oil; my cup runneth over.

Surely goodness and mercy shall follow me all the days of my life: and I will dwell in the house of the Lord forever.

—Psalm 23:4-6

Afterword

I personally witnessed all of the events described within this book. It is my firm belief that these scenarios occurred as a direct result of answer to prayer, or in powerful demonstration of Divine intervention in the forms of protection, guidance, healing and supply.

The reader, of course, may have—and is entitled to—another opinion. Some may contend that these circumstances which I described were merely every day coincidences.

Perhaps they are correct in that opinion. If so, then we must at least admit that my life has been an amazing collection of "coincidences."

In the final analysis, the position held regarding this book will be dictated by the individual's own belief system—that paradigm which best makes meaning and provides comfort in an otherwise challenging and confusing world.

A life of random choices and happenstance may be the preferred worldview of some. As for me, I take comfort in the promise that "the steps of a good man are ordered by the Lord, and he delights in his way."

—Psalm 37:23.

About the Author

Over the course of thirty years, Michael Hawron has had many unique adventures, in thirty countries on five continents. His decades of world travel began with a long break from his formal studies in behavioral sciences at the Alfred P. Sloan School of Management at the Massachusetts Institute of Technology. He completed his Master of Science degree in Higher Education and Adult Learning at Texas A&M University.

Michael has been attacked by baboons, survived natural disasters, and met a variety of colorful characters all over the globe. His first book, *Entertaining Detours*, is an insightful memoir and humorous look at his many unique adventures.

Hawron and his wife, Annette, live on a small farm in rural East Texas, the setting and source of the short stories contained in his heartwarming collection, *The Little Town with the Big Heart*.

Hawron is the father of twelve children and the grandfather of fifteen. His new spy thriller, *Just Good Clean Fun*, is his first published work of historical fiction, set in the turbulent 1970s–1980s.

Books by Michael Hawron:

Entertaining Detours

The Little Town with the Big Heart

Just Good Clean Fun

Awesome Footsteps

* * * * * *

For more information, photos, stories,
or fun facts and trivia:

Follow me on Facebook:
Entertaining Detours
or
Visit my website at:

www.mikehawron.com

Readers' comments and
Suggestions are **always** welcome!
Write to: mikehawronbooks@gmail.com

Made in the USA
Lexington, KY
19 February 2018